IN THE FOOTSTEPS
OF A
POLAR BEAR

A tribute to Captain James Erskine Knox

by his son Peter

i

Dedication

This book is unashamedly dedicated to my Father. Had his war injury proved fatal I very much doubt that I would be where I am today doing what I am doing with my wife, children, family and friends that I have. It was from his guidance that I became the person I am. I recall him telling me that there is no written rule book or school to teach parents how to bring up their children. With the first child, me, he said that he was very strict and with the second a lot more lenient and hopefully with the third he would get the balance right. I can only look at the results and certainly would not complain about him being over strict with me as it has served me well during my life.

So it is with eternal thanks that I dedicate this book to him for although to the world he was one of many - To me he was **My Father**.

Thanks To All Those That Helped

It is impossible to name all those that in some measure helped me in my journey. If your name does not appear below it is because of my memory not because your contribution did not warrant a mention, it did since it takes every piece of the jigsaw no matter how small to make a whole. The names are listed alphabetically not in any order of importance. As it says in Matthew 19:30 "The first shall be last and the last shall be first" and the only way I know to achieve that is if they all go together equally as one and so it is with those I have listed below and those I can't remember.

Cavalry Museum Amersfoort - Brother James Bonner - Ton Boots - Paul Bosonnet - Confuzzled – Jo Debnan - Wensley DeNiese - Wil van Elk - Freemasons Library for information regarding Jimmie's membership.- Michael & Norma Godfrey - Sid Godfrey - Joe Hoadly - Mrs M Holgate - Major Peter Howe - Professor Richard Holmes – Christopher Knox – Simon Knox - Reverend Stuart G Lee - Angela Mould - Phil Newbury - Mr AG (Bert) Parsons - Gwyn Petty - Audrey Pounds - Mrs D Quare - Paul Reed - Will & Joze Rutten-Nass - Paul Sanders - Lee Smith - Margot Smolenaars - Petra M Steenvoorde-Brussen - Peter Wilms - Wimbledon Museum of Local History

Author's Note

All the characters mentioned by name in this book were real people and their character has been faithfully presented from either personal knowledge or the available historic information. Any resemblance to other people bearing the same name is purely coincidental.

CONTENTS

Foreword

If it was not for two people Mr R. Pulle and "Confuzzled" the probability is that this story may never have been told. I have not met either and as far as I am aware the two have never met.

It was Mr R Pulle whose ambition was to have a souvenir from the war. He remembered that on 16th April 1945 when his local village of Loenen was liberated the lead armoured car was hit by a Panzerfaust. In the cleanup of the war detritus after the liberation its burnt-out remains were dumped in the woods behind an attractive thatched house then called Klein Iwalt (Little Iwalt) now known as De Lijster & de Linde (The Thrush & the Linden Tree). The house is situated on the east side of the Cemetery on Groenendaalseweg.

On the 15th August 1945, the car still remained in the woods behind De Lijster & de Linde so Mr Reinier Johnannes Cornelis Pulle and his son Frederik Anton Pulle decided to liberate it. Off they went one day with a wheelbarrow, toolbox and a length of rope and dismantled the gun from the turret. They placed the gun in the wheelbarrow and with the father pulling using the rope and the son pushing and steering the wheelbarrow they managed to take it to De Looijenboom their home on Groenendaalseweg.

He built a Cairn in his garden on top of which he proudly mounted the gun. After 33 years resting in the garden his son, Maarten thought that it would be an idea to use the gun as a memorial in the town centre and unveil it as part of the celebrations for the 40th anniversary of their liberation. As you will read this came to fruition with many Polar Bears including my Father, Jimmie attending the unveiling.

Upon Jimmie's return to the UK, I was interested to know all about his visit since like a lot of old soldiers he rarely talked about his experiences in the war. Given that he was in a Reconnaissance Regiment he was very sketchy on exactly where he had been. He gave me two pieces of information. Firstly they were near a large town called Apeldoorn and secondly the name De Brink. Later in the year I was collecting a Mercedes from their factory in Sindelfingen in Germany and decided that I would visit the Memorial on the way home. Nothing could be easier I had the information from a Captain in the Recce. Nothing could be further from the truth! I did not find it in on my return as I had hoped and spent many subsequent years returning to the area searching out all the De Brinks I found on Google Earth. I also travelled many a mile with the Golden man along Dutch roads looking but without success. Not to be beaten I embraced the global services of the internet and posted a question with only the information that I had. This is when the second person entered into the frame I know not his name just his nom de plume, Confuzzled. To this person I remain deeply thankful for without his help whilst history would still be there I would not have been able to follow in the Footsteps of a Polar Bear. He, for I assume that they were a he, provided that all-important missing link that enabled me to find a Paul Sanders in Loenen, Holland and Sid Godfrey, a Polar Bear, from Arundel in West Sussex. They helped to open up my world to so many more wonderful and helpful people that in turn have opened up the hidden story of my Father's life. It means so much more to me and also to his grandchildren than just the few snapshots of his experiences that he divulged.

The events in this story are as accurate as the information that I have uncovered and have been joined together with my imagination knowing my parents as I did. If readers find any discrepancy in the facts or can add to my story I would be pleased to know.

Contact me at:-

jek.polarbear@gmail.com

Now come with me and follow in the footsteps of a Polar Bear on my journey of discovery.

PART ONE

Preparation

Chapter 1   The Early Days

In the southwest of London, there is an area called Cottenham Park situated about a mile and a half away from Raynes Park Station just four stations away from Waterloo on the mainline from Portsmouth. In the first decade of the twentieth Century, Cottenham Park was on the outer reaches of London where the countryside began. The leafiness of the countryside was achieved by the planting of the hardy Plane Tree at intervals along the pavement edge with the road. Its khaki camouflage-patterned bark was caused by the tree shedding its old polluted bark. Even the leaves were self-cleaning of the soot and smoke from the open fires prevalent in the new suburbia leaving the trees a bright clean green. In a suburban street of Cottenham Park called Spencer Road, there is one particular red brick built suburban house where our story starts.

On the 27th of April 1917, the first cries were heard that heralded the birth of a Polar Bear. The midwife and the mother did not recognise it as a Polar Bear. As far as they were concerned it was just the crying of a newborn, the third child and the first son born to Rosetta Knox. It was to be 23 years and in another war that the transformation was to take place. The First World War was in its final albeit still bloody stages which meant that the Father was not pacing the room below waiting for the news of his wife's delivery, instead he was hundreds of miles away. Having recovered from a phosgene attack at Wulverghem he was now fighting near Messines on the Western Front. The first he knew was when he read the published Orders No 124 of 5th Battalion East Surrey Regiment on 4th June 1917. They read that a son was born to the wife of 200753 CSM J.E.Knox 'B' Coy on 27th April 1917". A few days later on the 7th June he would witness the largest man-made non-nuclear explosions on the Messines Ridge.

The day before he had received this good news his son had been taken to St Matthews the CofE Church situated at the opposite end of Spencer Road where it joined with Durham Road. The Church like many things managed to survive until the Second World War when at 8.30 in the morning of St Peter's Day, the 29th of June 1944 it was destroyed by a V1 flying bomb. He was christened as James Erskine Knox after his Father, his Grandfather and Great-grandfather before him; a line of James Erskines going back one hundred years. Father and son were not to meet until the middle of September after the East Surreys were relieved and withdrawn from the front line.

His family of Dorothy and Phyllis was completed when his third and baby sister, christened Olive, was born on the 23rd July 1919. His Father after volunteering for the services, serving in South Africa and then France for the whole of the First World was finally demobbed on 15th November 1919. He returned home and found employment as a Maintenance Engineer for a local company.

His father served six years in the service of the King and achieved the rank of Company Sergeant Major so it would be expected for discipline and attention to detail to prevail in his house. Certainly there was the essence of Victorian etiquette. You weren't allowed to call on friends without an appointment and never before ten in the morning, a rule that Jimmie adhered to the rest of his life and installed onto his children who still follow the rule in principle. No guests were allowed in the house until the ladies were properly attired in both dress and makeup and this was something that his sisters strongly adhered to even in the more laid back times of the 1980s.

There are some child psychologists that think the first child follows the rules and the second is the wild card. Certainly this played out with the two older sisters but given Jimmie was the first son albeit the third child how would he develop? During his early years he was a fairly typical child vying with his siblings for his parent's attention. Sundays would be spent dressed in their Sunday best, attending church and then after the traditional roast, they would take a walk in Holland Gardens, a public park at the top end of his road where it joined Cottenham Park Road. The park was fenced off with metal railings with only two gates. It had flower beds with benches interspersed between them that looked over a large open green space so it was a safe area for little Jimmie to stretch his young legs.

It was in 1921 when he went to school that things changed. He mixed with other children and started to understand that there was another way to do things rather than that of his parent's. By this time his parents had moved to a small house in Pepys Road just a short walk from where they used to live whilst remaining in the area of Cottenham Park. Number 68 was a centre property of a group of terraced houses positioned just after the large detached houses built in the prime positions close to the railway station of Raynes Park. It was a red brick-built house of the two up, two down tradition with a kitchen extended out the back of the house with a scullery linking it to the back garden where there was an outside toilet. With four children it was a bit crowded however since Jimmie was the only boy he had a bedroom upstairs all to himself that overlooked the back garden.

Fortunately at the end of Pepys Road was a suitable school. In the days before the 1944 Education Act it was called an Elementary School as the then current educational thinking claimed that elementary was the only education most people needed. The school was situated next to the local GPO sorting office and was called the Cottenham Park Elementary School. It was a co-educational school taking children up to the age of eleven. It was there that he first discovered the two essentials of his early education; the requirement of having to learn and the cane. Cottenham Park School was in two buildings, there was the original Victorian brick built building which contained the Head Master's office and staff room as well as classrooms for the third and fourth-year students. At the rear of this building on the south side of the playground was the school hall, a temporary large single room built in 1898 made from clad corrugated iron. In 1907 to cater for the increased number of children it was converted into three individual classrooms. At the time the H.M. Inspectors for Schools recommended that more permanent premises should receive the attention of the school Governors. True to form 68 years and two World Wars later it happened and consequently was of no benefit to Jimmie.

School for Jimmie was a newly found freedom; he could walk there on his own and walk home although there were times when the return journey was very long. Part of this was because his new best friend George Childs lived a few doors down towards the school and he would stop off there on the way home. As time went by the return trips from school began to involve a little wandering. As the years went by the wandering became further afield. During the long summer holidays the pair of them found the apple and cherry orchards on the other side of the railway line.

This was a wonderful adventure. They could climb trees and make camps. The apples and cherries were too much of a temptation for little boys. Sometimes they got away with climbing the trees and pinching apples. Other times just as Jimmie was lowering himself out of a tree to the ground a strong right arm would lift him up again so that he was face high with the farmer. A thick ear was the order of the day.

If they spotted the farmer coming they would run as fast as they could. The trouble was that their reputation preceded them; the farmer knew where they lived. Whilst he was eating his tea there would be a knock at the door. "Your son's been in my orchard again" he would hear the farmer say and he knew what would happen next. Sometimes it was less painful to get caught by the farmer.

As he got older so his pranks became more adventurous. In the 1920s the safety match was rare. The most common match was a red match which you could strike by friction alone. Jimmie found that if he carefully scraped the red combustible head off the end of the match, wrap it tightly in the foil of a milk bottle top and then hit it with a hammer it would go off with a bang. By experimentation he found that the loudness of the noise depended on the number of match heads and the tightness of the foil. So far so good, but there had to be another way of making it explode rather than just hitting it with a hammer.

Now at the bottom of his road the trams rattled their way from Wimbledon to Kingston and back. They came along Worple Road and skewed into the bottom part of Pepys Road to run past his school. It was an awkward junction so the trams had to slow down and proceed carefully around the bend. This opened up the opportunity for an excellent prank. So he carefully crammed as many match head scrapings as he possibly could into the confines of one milk bottle top. He had never made one quite so big before. This should be a cracker he thought and set off for the bottom of the road. He stood at the junction, milk bottle top bomb in his hand and watched as the trams swayed around the bend. He decided he knew the best place to put his bomb. All he had to do now was to wait until a tram was approaching, place his bomb on the rail, retire a little and watch

The next tram came, the bomb was placed. The tram got closer and closer, it swayed one way and back just as the wheels ran over the milk bottle top. The explosion was louder than he expected. The tram driver was taken aback and performed an emergency stop. The passengers on board were surprised and shocked. What had happened? The Ticket collector climbed down and went to see for himself, half expecting the wheel to have fallen off. Crowds gathered. Jimmie thought this was great and couldn't help but chuckle out loud. That was the best prank ever, he thought.

Unfortunately his Head Master who lived not far down the road was attracted to find out what the noise and kerfuffle were all about. Once again Jimmie's notoriety preceded him and when the Head Master saw him chuckling away put two and two together. The next day at school he was hauled into the Head Master's study to see if a whacking could make more noise.

Jimmie slowly came to his senses. He eventually worked out that his bravado over not handing in his homework and all his pranks was not worth it as the pain exceeded the pleasure. He started to take a more serious approach to his education. This did not mean that he gave up playing pranks; he just became a lot better at improving his ability to escape the blame as we will discover later.

As scrumping was off the agenda George and he turned their attentions in the direction of Wimbledon Common a short albeit uphill walk taking ten minutes or so. Wimbledon common was an open heathland stretching from the top of Wimbledon Hill to join with Putney Heath to the north and to the west through a more wooded area as far as Beverley Brook. Even in the 1920s the area was protected, supposedly sporting some unique species of natural flora and fauna including a reputation for being a most prolific area for the Stag Beetle, the largest terrestrial insect in Europe; new and better opportunities opened up.

The immediate interest to the two boys was not the open heathland with its ponds but the ancient wooded area known to them as Caesars Camp. Although he didn't know at the time to get to the campsite he walked past a couple of houses on the appropriately named road of Campside that had been built by his Grandfather. Had he looked up he would have seen his mark on the topping out stone.

The two boys were more interested in the remains of an Iron Age hill fort. Although they didn't fully appreciate the evidence that it was stormed and captured by the *Legio II Augusta* under Vespasian in his push westwards in AD 44 as part of the invasion of Britain ordered by Claudius. The boys just knew it as Caesar's camp and from that the fertile imagination of the two boys ran riot. One day they would be the ancient Britons defending their town from attack and then they would become Roman soldiers guarding the stone well that was sunk in a hollow within a circle of trees. They would often venture deeper into the woods, one day finding the fast running but relatively shallow Beverly Brook or they would roam northwards towards Putney where they found a Windmill. It had been left abandoned and unworkable in 1864 when the miller was evicted. He was the victim of an ambitious landowner that wanted to develop the common for his own gains. The development was not approved and because the miller took all the key working parts with him the windmill still remained unworkable as a reminder of the outcome. Again the history of the mill was not in the conscious mind of the boys it was just a fascinating construction. They would stand beneath and gaze up at the huge sails on the Windmill and perhaps even enjoy a bit of internal exploration.

With the Rushmore pond on Wimbledon Common close by a boy handy with his hands would not be a boy without a boat. And so he would spend many hours standing by the pond waiting patiently for the breeze to bring his boat to shore. There were times when just as his boat approached the wind shifted and his boat would jybe and go sailing away. "Honest mum it did".

It must have been at about this time that he thought a Tattoo was the thing to have. So he took his steel nib dipping pen, opened his bottle of ink and started to give himself a tattoo. It was to be an anchor but he did not get far just the claws and part of the shank before his parents found out. His ambitions of an anchor left him with what looked like a letter "m" permanently on his forearm.

Jimmie settled down to his academic life a little more fervently than hitherto and in 1928 JE Junior entered Wimbledon Central, regarded as the best Elementary School in the area. The school was two miles away from home being situated in South Wimbledon towards the boundary with Merton. At that time there was no direct public transport connection so he would have to set off early in the morning for his 40 minute walk into school.

Judged by the standard of his first school Wimbledon Central was wonderful. The building with its ornate Georgian style architecture was opened in 1909 as Pelham School by the Lord Chief Justice of England who described it as "The most magnificent school". There was no school within 20 miles to rival it. It had all modern amenities, a service lift, a 100 foot high bell tower and running water from its own 1000 gallon cistern housed in the tower. In 1927, just before Jimmie joined, the school had a name change and became Wimbledon Central under the headship of Mr Burton. In 1957, when his second son Graham, following in his father's footsteps, attended the school it had reverted back to its original name of Pelham. In July 1983 academia left the building and it was converted into flats where it is possible that some of the earlier students now as senior citizens occupy its rooms.

Not only was the building "magnificent" the teaching facilities were as well and Jimmie found the woodworking classes thoroughly enjoyable, they helped to develop the skills of his genes. His grandfather was a fine woodcarver being responsible for the carving of the oak seats of the chancel and the aumbry door in Westminster Cathedral. Although in his life he was to take a different route to a trade in woodworking the skills he learned at school enabled him to build some rather nice pieces of furniture that he made from the hard wood blocks used in the printing trade. When he moved into his first and only house in Grand Drive he designed and made the fitted kitchen; the joints and his skill set a high standard for the subsequent off the shelf products to achieve.

As the '20s turned into the '30s the great depression underway in the United States was rippling across the pond to the United Kingdom to become the largest and most profound economic depression of the 20th Century. Although the school leaving age was still officially fourteen at Wimbledon Central they encouraged the children to remain until they attained the age of 15. As 1932 dawned Jimmie's academic career headed towards its conclusion and the country moved towards the depth of the Great Slump, as it was known. With 3.5 million registered unemployed and many more in part-time work, although mostly in the industrial heartlands of Britain, it was not going to be easy for young Jimmie to get a job. Although he had made an improved effort in his academic studies a Cert A was not within his grasp. There was no chance of him going into any form of further education and because of the massive unemployment at the time it was going to be difficult to enter the trades as his Grandfather and Great-grandfather had done. He joined the many hopefuls in searching for employment opportunities advertised in the newspapers and from the list available at what was then called the Unemployment Offices.

His searching paid off, he found a job in London and at the age of 15 Jimmie left school and entered into the world of commerce. On 5th June 1932 he started work at Sardinia House in Holborn not far from Fleet Street and the City of London. He joined, as a Junior Clerk, a technical journal called the Electrical Times, which was then a member of the Iliffe Group. The company was producing a small black and white A5 booklet especially for the electricity supply companies. This started his life in print which apart from an interruption to escort Hitler's troops back to Germany meant a daily commute into London until he warranted the perk of a company car.

Jimmie circa 1922

Chapter 2   *Friends for Life*

With the death of the elderly German President, Paul von Hindenburg, at his country estate in East Prussia, a well prepared Hitler embraced this opportunity to seize total power in Germany. The road was even now more firmly set on the way to the expansion of Germany's authority, or should that be Hitler's, and the eventual tumble into conflict.

A long time before Hitler had any ambitions of extending the might of the German Empire drill halls came into existence in the UK. They were used to create a reserve of men trained in fighting on the same lines as the regular army. Many of the drill halls were built in the Victorian period to accommodate local Rifle Volunteer Troops funded by either public subscription or local benefactors. In 1880 such a hall was built at 17A St Georges Road, Wimbledon in the South West of London. At the outbreak of war in 1914 it became the headquarters for the 5th Battalion East Surrey Regiment (A to G Companies.) of the Territorial Forces and one of those soldiers was J.E.Knox, Jimmie's father.

The Drill Hall was situated on the south side of St Georges Road and reached as far back as the main railway line to Waterloo. It was an impressive brick-built building with offices and accommodation for the instructor or caretaker at the front with an armoury behind them. At the back was a very large hall used for all types of training including rifle target practice.

The clouds of war started to darken once again over Europe. Jimmie, as had his father before him, wanted to be involved in the action and as he was now 17 years old he could enlist. On Tuesday 29th May 1934 on his way home from work in London he alighted at Wimbledon Station. He came out of the station crossed over the road and turned right towards Wimbledon Hill. He passed

Lloyds Bank and came to the junction with St Georges Road. He turned left and as a tram rattled past him he reached 17A. The door was open and welcoming. He stepped inside, it was dark compared to the outside and before his eyes got accustomed to the change his nostrils were attacked by the smell of a mixture of wooden floors wax polish and spent cordite. This was the same building that his father had reported to over twenty years before and the coincidence was not lost on him nor did they stop there.

He found an old soldier, the RSM as it turned out and said that he wanted to join up. On giving him his name the RSM looked at him and asked

"Are you any relation to CSM James Erskine Knox of "B" Company the 5th battalion of the East Surrey Regiment?"

"He is my Father"

"I served with him during the last fracas; you have a lot to live up to young man"

"I know. I will not let him down, nor my King or Country"

The RSM completed the Army Form E501, Identification on Enlistment and then took him to see the recruiting officer 2nd Lieutenant Ronald Hatton who completed the remainder of the form. Jimmie proudly added his signature giving a commitment to four years of service in the Territorial Army and at the same time attesting that he had accepted the service conditions. He also took the oath of allegiance saying.

> **"I James Erskine Knox, swear by Almighty God that I will be faithful and bear true allegiance to His Majesty King George the Fifth, His Heirs and Successors, and that I**

will, as in duty bound, honestly and faithfully defend His Majesty, His Heirs, and Successors, in Person, Crown, and Dignity against all enemies, according to the conditions of my service."

He walked proudly home and had to wait until the 4th June 1934 to be informed that his application was approved. He had accomplished the first objective in following in his Father's footsteps. JEK junior was now in the army serving as 6140513 committed to an initial period of 4 years in the 5th Battalion of the East Surrey Regiment, "B" Company, exactly the same as his father before him.

It must be a common family trait as he threw himself enthusiastically into this new adventure. He attended the maximum number of drill days at the Wimbledon Drill Hall undergoing his initial training and learning to become a soldier. Square bashing and rifle drill taught timing and coordination. If he knew up from down when he joined he may not know it now. All he knew was that if he was ordered to do something he would react instinctively. He learnt what it meant to be a soldier and how the Army functions. He was also taught survival and field-craft skills, first aid, and how to use a rifle. Plus his physical fitness and stamina were built up. By the 8th of July he was accepted as fully trained. Private Knox J E was on his way.

His first annual camp occurred not long after he was accepted as fully trained. Camps were spent at various Army camps in the south of England. Nowadays with improved cars and motorways places like Arundel Park, Salisbury Plain, Longmoor and also in 1936 at Shorncliffe (where he was to return some years later for officer training) are just a short drive away. For a London born boy brought up albeit on the edges of the "big smoke" the camps took a long time to get to and seemed to be deep in the countryside. It would be impossible to argue that he did not like the camps as every year between 1934 and 1939 he would spend 15 days, the maximum number permitted.

1935 was the Silver Jubilee year for King George V and Jimmie was involved in the celebrations of 6th May when he took part in the local parade. On the following day he also took part in the Service of thanksgiving at the All England Tennis grounds. He also participated on the 22nd January 1936 in the Proclamation ceremony for Edward VIII and again later that year after the abdication he was also present on 12th December for the proclamation of George VI.

1935 saw him become interested in boxing, fighting as a lightweight he had more than a modest amount of success judging by the number of cups that graced his shelves at home. Unfortunately all the hard fought for cups ended up as part of a burglar's swag in 1969 and were never recovered. It was on the occasion of the East Surrey Regiment's boxing championships held at his drill hall on the Wednesday evening15[th] January 1936 he fought his last match as a Private. The first round went in his favour when he beat Boswell from "D" Company (Epsom & Leatherhead) on points. His opponent in the final was Collier from his own "B" Company who had also won against Feltham of "C" Company (Sutton) on points. The opening round of the final went to Jimmie. In the second round Collier fought back causing Jimmie to take some heavy punishment. In the third round both went to it with a will and there was little to choose between them. Alas Collier won the cup. Although the championship went to "B" Company his was obviously not the result that he wanted, however, as some compensation the next day Jimmie was told he had been awarded his first stripe; he was promoted to Lance Corporal.

This was the first rung on the ladder, a small one perhaps but it was probably the most difficult. This is where you stop being a private, a squaddie, one of us and become one of them. It is where from being in the ranks you have the first opportunity to supervise four of your previously fellow privates in what was known as a section. Last week you were one of the lads with your moans and gripes about officers and their ways. Now you are poacher turned gamekeeper. You have to lead, manage, give orders and what is probably initially the most difficult, to ensure that the orders given from above are carried out no matter your own personal view. The other advantage is that it opens up opportunities to specialise and undertake specialist military training and in two months he had qualified as a machine gun instructor.

Eleven stations out of London in the easterly direction on the line to Gravesend is a station called Belvedere. Belvedere is from the Italian meaning beautiful view and was given to the area by the philanthropist and reformer Sir Culling Eardley when he built his house in the 1770s on the high ground overlooking the Thames. With the arrival of the North Kent Railway the area was developed into an industrial area and the riverside hamlet of Picardy became Lower Belvedere and boasted the station of Belvedere. The area around the station spreading south of Lower Road reaching back towards Abbey Wood and onwards towards Erith was developed as a settlement of terraced cottages for workers at the nearby factories and wharves on the marshland bordering the river. One of the roads that went into this developing industrial area was Crabtree Manorway (More recently the top end of Crabtree Manorway at the junction with Lower Road has been renamed as Mitchell Close) and on that junction was a general store come tobacconist and newsagent and next door a greengrocers. The name over the shops was A.G. Parsons.

The owner Albert George Parsons with his wife and two children, another Albert George and Anne who everyone called Nancy, lived in a large three bedroomed flat over the shops. In the late summer of 1936 Albert George junior, or Bert as he was called, decided to visit a cousin who lived in Russell Road, Wimbledon which branched off the Broadway adjacent to the Wimbledon Theatre. During his visit he was recommended to stretch his legs and lungs on Wimbledon Common. The common was only a mile away although he didn't know it at the time half a mile was uphill; he set out on foot. It was a pleasant sunny day and with all the deep breathing his throat got dry. On the way to the common he noticed a pub at the end of the parade of shops leading to the common. He decided before he set off on the return journey he would wet his whistle. The pub was associated with the Dog and Fox Hotel. Bert entered and went up to the bar that took up almost the whole length of the room. As he approached the bartender who had been chatting to a customer at the other end came over and asked him what he wanted.

"I'll have a pint of your local brew please"

"That will be Young's Best then, it's brewed not far from here in Wandsworth. We get a delivery every day so it's always in its prime." The barman continued "They still use a dray pulled up here by two large light grey shires so it's a nice steady trip, the beer is not shaken about as it is on the back of a lorry."

He had finished pulling the pint and placed it on the bar for Bert. "That'll be 8 pence please sir."

Bert gave him a tanner and a threepenny bit receiving one penny in change.

"I take it you are not from around here then?" asked the barman

The man at the other end of the bar looked up.

"I'm from the other side of London a place called Belvedere in Kent. I'm up here visiting my cousin"

"You enjoy our beer then when you get back home you can tell them how great it is"

Bert left the bar and looked for a vacant table to give his feet and legs a rest. He chose one over by the window so he could watch the passers-by. He had a few sips of his beer, his attention drawn by the dress of those in the street outside. The ladies were mostly smartly attired and the men could have been bankers or city types. There wasn't a cloth cap to be seen except when a delivery lorry trundled past.

"Do you like it then?" he heard a voice say.

He looked up and standing before him was the young man he had seen at the other end of the bar.

"Sorry" he continued "my name is Jimmie do you mind if I join you?"

"By all means" replied Bert indicating a chair.

Little did either of them know at the time how much that short conversation was going to change their lives. Jimmie sat down and the conversation between them started and continued only being stopped whilst first Jimmie bought a round and later reciprocated by Bert. The two of them just seemed to hit it off. When the time came to go home Jimmie offered to walk down the hill with him and somewhere on that walk an offer was made by Bert for Jimmie to come and stay at Belvedere. The offer was accepted and a date agreed upon. When they reached Ely's Corner where Worple Road met Wimbledon Hill they shook hands and with a date set for his visit Jimmie turned right into Worple Road and home whilst Bert carried on towards the Broadway and his cousin's.

The agreed weekend duly arrived so on Saturday morning he added a couple of clean shirts to his overnight case and set off. He went to Waterloo as usual and instead of stepping out across Waterloo Bridge in the direction of the Aldwych and Sardinia House he crossed Waterloo Road and into Waterloo East Station. He bought a weekend return ticket to Belvedere. The first stop was London Bridge and then it was into uncharted areas, he did recognise the name of Woolwich Arsenal although he had never visited there. Stations came and stations went, he knew the journey would take forty minutes. After ten stations the train pulled into Abbey Wood the station before Belvedere. As the train pulled out of Abbey Wood Jimmie got himself ready to get off at the next stop. The train began to slow down and the clank-clank clank-clank of the carriages' bogies as they ran over the join in the rails after the level crossing slowed to a stop as they came to a halt alongside the platform. Case in hand he alighted and followed a few other passengers to the left for the exit. As promised Bert was waiting for him with a welcoming handshake. They decided to walk rather than take the trolley bus as it was only less than a mile. Once again the couple found conversation easy between them as they walked. On the left was a large allotment area beside the road where the locals who only had small handkerchief sized gardens could grow their own vegetables to help supplement their income. The horizon behind them was dominated by the powerhouse supplying the engine manufacturing works of the Ford Motor Company in Dagenham on the other side of the River Thames. On the right as they walked were a series of terraced houses set up above the road level. It wasn't long before they arrived at the shop. Bert turned down Crabtree Manorway explaining that the shops were open and may have customers so for ease they would use the back entrance.

Along the side of the property was an iron railing behind which was a narrow strip garden just over an arm's length wide planted with a variety of bushes. The grass between them Jimmie noted could do with a cut. A full height blue painted wooden door opened into the rear garden although Jimmie thought that it was a bit more like a yard. On the left hand side was a neat small lawn with three sides planted out as a border. It ran the full width of the wall of the Pentecostal Church next door. Beyond the garden was a paved path which Jimmie was to discover later lead to various storage sheds. To the right was another large paved area leading up to the back of the house. In front of him a couple of steps led up to the entrance of what turned out to be their dining room which also had direct access into the greengrocer's shop at the front. Just to the right was a set of steps leading down into a cellar. At the first floor level was a large bay window and he could just make out a chaise longue on the left hand side. The right side, the house was extended rearwards and this area contained the kitchen. It was through the kitchen door that Bert beckoned Jimmie. Inside was an older woman who Bert introduced as his Mother. For a woman she was quite tall, certainly taller than his mother but not as tall as him. She had grey hair in a tight perm which made her appear old but her skin was of a younger person.

"Take Jimmie up to his room and I'll make him a cup of tea. I'm sure he could do with one. Dad's in the dining room behind the shop and your sister is making good the stock in the shop ready for the lunchtime rush."

There was a long corridor towards the front with a door at the end which opened into the general stores. The stairs doubled back on the corridor ending to the side of the large bay window he had observed from outside. "Bathrooms on the left" Bert said "and you are kipping in my room just here. They have put me on a camp bed in the front room. Make yourself at home and when you are ready come down to the kitchen, mum makes a mean cup of tea."

Once Jimmie had sorted himself out and had a bit of a wash and bush up he made his way down the stairs. The door to the shop was now open and he could see a pair of calves coming out of a pair of flat comfortable shoes. As he came down the stairs the picture before him began to show more of the person to whom the legs belonged. Did they belong to Bert's sister Anne, who for some reason never discovered, was called Nancy, he wondered? Just at that moment they moved off to the left and disappeared. When he reached the bottom instead of turning left and along the corridor he walked straight into the shop. Fortunately there were no customers. Standing before him checking the shelves were full was a 17 year old girl. It was the same person as he had a partial view of as he came down the stairs. The dress of which he had only glimpsed a fraction of before was a light floral printed cotton dress with a round neckline and finished just below her knees. The sleeves were short with an elasticated hem that gave them a puffed effect. Her hair was a rich middle brown and was as the fashion dictated, permed into a series of six or seven waves as it came over her head from a right side parting. The shorter side just having three waves to balance the effect. She smiled, he smiled and as they say the rest was to become history.

Bert was a good Mein Host and he took him to see some of the interesting places locally including the Half Way House his local just a short walk there and a longer stagger back. The rest of the time was spent with Nancy. They walked and talked through the fields down towards the river. On Sunday afternoon the shop was closed and after a roast lunch the whole family walked up Poplar Mount to Frank's Park where a local brass ensemble's tunes echoed across the short cut grass from the bandstand at its centre. They returned home to tea and sandwiches and then it was time for Jimmie to depart.

Both Nancy and Bert accompanied him to the station and as the train came into the station they made their farewells Jimmie's ending with a promise wrapped up in two words, "I'll write".

It was back to work with a bump on Monday and the Drill hall on Wednesday. The following weekend he penned his promise to Nancy. More visits to 239 Lower Road and Frank's Park were made over the next year, perhaps not as many as Nancy would have liked since the Army seemed to have the first call on his time. His reward from the army was to gain his second stripe as Corporal on 21st March 1938. Not only was his ability being recognised by the TA his love life was also blossoming with Nancy. His 21st birthday fell on a Wednesday, Drill night, so he spent the latter part of the evening with the guys of his platoon drinking at The Alexandra. Saturday he was with Nancy. Taking seriously the responsibility that came with reaching the age of majority, Jimmie asked Nancy to marry him. His diary records his feelings for he wrote,

"I cannot believe how lucky I am that such a beautiful girl has agreed to marry me".

The ring that sealed the beginning of their life together was a seven stone diamond cluster.

Jimmie (21) Engaged to Nancy (19)

Chapter 3   Call to the Colours

Whilst Hitler was strengthening his armed forces and extending his control into Austria and Czechoslovakia on the pretext that they were mistreating some of his countrymen, Jimmie continued with his soldiering. In May 1938 four years had passed since he signed up. He was enjoying his army life and with the threat of war still on the horizon, he signed up for another year.

After another fifteen days at camp his third stripe was confirmed. He was now Sergeant Jimmie Knox making both him and his parents, especially his father very proud of his achievement. This was the third step on the ladder and one that made him second in command of a platoon of up to 35 soldiers. It also carried the important responsibility for advising and assisting junior officers. August 1938 was an important month for him, the culmination of over 4 years of hard training was rewarded with him proudly receiving his Territorial Army Badge number 86160.

Hitler in the meantime was continuing to his own aggressive agenda still threatening to intervene in Czechoslovakia. Seeking a peaceful solution the then prime minister Neville Chamberlain met with Adolf Hitler in Munich in September. He returned waving a piece of paper declaring "I believe it is peace in our time".

After years of appeasement and peace seeking the UK armed services were under strength and the equipment insufficient and outdated. Towards the end of 1938 the Territorial Army was ordered to double its strength. A second line regiment, known as the 67th (East Surrey) Anti-Tank, Royal Artillery was formed, partly from Jimmie's 5th battalion and the rest from new recruits. So without having to do anything on 28th November Jimmie's role changed from infantry to the Royal Artillery as his unit was re-designated as the 226th of 57th Anti Tank Regt. The then

Secretary of State for War, Lesley Hore-Belisha, visited the Wimbledon Drill Hall where he emphasised the importance of the change by saying

> *"Famous infantry battalions like your own are thus invited to assume another task – a task that will demand all your application and all your energies which you have hitherto devoted to your work in the line"*

Eagerly applying himself to the new task at hand another year soon passed and on 14th March he keenly signed on for another year making it 6 years service in total. He was later to receive a medal and bar for his long service. June saw another re-designation of his unit to the 266th of 67th Anti Tank Regt. Then on 1st July 1939 he received another promotion, this time to the provisional rank of Battery Quartermaster Sergeant (BQMS). This he considered a great achievement, as he was now the same rank that his father held during the First World War. In August he was at camp again in Tilshead on Salisbury Plain.

After all his training with the rifle, general machine gun and the Bren he now had to turn his learning and training skills onto the attack of Tanks and other armoured vehicles. This involved the recognition of the variety of German armoured vehicles and the strength and position of the armour on the vehicle. The main anti-tank weapon in use by the army was designed by Captain Henry C Boys during the interwar period. It was his idea of dealing with the new menace on the battlefield, the tank. For all intents and purposes it was a big rifle, 25% longer than the infantry's 303 Lee Enfield it weighed in at 16 Kg and was capable of firing a 0.55 (14 mm) bullet. Like the LE303 it was a bolt action fed from a 5 round detachable box magazine mounted on the top. As can be imagined it had a kick like a mule and if not handled correctly could cause neck strains and bruised shoulders. Jimmie's boxing training enabled him to cope with the extra kick and he soon mastered it becoming very proficient in its use and the training of troops. It was initially called the Stanchion but was renamed the Boys Anti Tank rifle as a mark of respect for the designer who died a few days before it was approved for service. The Boys was replaced in 1943 by another British designed anti-tank weapon, the Projector, Infantry, Anti Tank Mk I; more commonly known by its acronym of PIAT.

The clouds of war were deepening over Europe. In preparation for what was inevitable on the 1st September a telegram was received at the Regiment HQ, Wimbledon with instructions to embody. Messages went out immediately to all officers and the general call to the colours was confirmed by Radio broadcasts. With a feeling of excitement insomuch that he will now have the opportunity to see if all his hard work and training will actually work in practice. He said goodbye to his parents and three sisters took his kit bag and on the 2nd of September Jimmie, reported for duty at the drill hall in Wimbledon. When he reported he was welcomed by the news that his provisional rank of Battery Quartermaster Sergeant had been confirmed. Wimbledon was one of the first Companies to report that it was complete.

The next day, Sunday 3rd September 1939, had time run out for any peaceful settlement with Hitler? At 11 o'clock in the morning everybody crowded around the wireless sets in silence. When the chimes of Big Ben had rung out eleven times the country silently listened to find out.

"This is the BBC. Here is the Prime Minister the Right Honourable Neville Chamberlain."

"I am speaking to you from the Cabinet Room of 10 Downing Street. This morning the British Ambassador in Berlin handed the German Government a final note stating that unless we heard from them by 11 o'clock that they were prepared at once to withdraw their troops from Poland a state of war would exist between us. I have to tell you now that no such undertaking has been received and that consequently this country is at war with Germany."

And so it was that a year after he returned from Munich waving that now infamous piece of white paper declaring "I believe it is peace in our time" that Chamberlain had declared War on his co-signatory. The "phoney war", as it was described, lasted for the first eight months of the war. It was a period when not a lot happened. The period was mostly used to get Britain prepared. Led by an appeasing Prime Minister one of the first tasks set for the RAF was to fly over Germany and drop thousands of "Letters to the German People" This had little effect apart from inviting Germany to increase her anti-aircraft defences.

The North Downs in the south west corner of England stretch from Farnham in the west to the white cliffs of Dover in the east. Epsom Downs, famous for the Derby horse race, forms a part of this low ridge of chalk hills and is located south west of London. On the 4th of September Jimmie's "B" Company was joined by "A" from Streatham, "C" from Sutton and "D" from Epsom and Leatherhead as the Regiment assembled on Epsom Downs to start their effort in the preparation for the defence of Britain.

The grandstand the highest structure on the downs provided excellent views over the Thames Valley from London in the northeast stretching round to the Chiltern Hills that shield Oxford from direct sight to the northwest.

But as they were to find out this lonely sentinel provided no respite in the winter from the racing wind and chilling cold that it brought. It was not unheard of for sentries to suffer from exposure and have to be rushed to the local hospital. The Sergeants needed no encouragement to seek out their own refuge and quickly denoted the local Derby Arms public house as their mess. For the first few days great emphasis was placed on basic training and self-defence, as well as passive air defence measures involving sandbagging, trench digging and manning anti-aircraft Bren gun posts. All in all it was a busy time.

After two weeks he requested and was granted a weekend pass and he set off for home and his fiancé, on what was to become a life-changing weekend. Nancy and he agreed to get married. So with much confusion in both of their families on Saturday 16th September he made a mad dash from Raynes Park to Belvedere to obtain a license and arrange details with the local catholic priest, Malachais Manley. Nancy was a Roman Catholic and she wanted to get married in a Catholic Church. Father Manley insisted that before he would grant permission as Jimmie was CofE that he had to get some undertakings. One of the undertakings was that any issue was to be brought up as Roman Catholics. To this and his other promises he held true. He managed to acquire a licence so on Sunday afternoon the 17th of September. With no time to organise a white wedding dress, Nancy attired in her Sunday Best left her home in Lower Road. Accompanied by her parents and Jimmie's sister Olive as her bridesmaid they travelled the couple of miles by trolley bus, to St Fidelis Church in West Street, Erith.

The church was small, brick-built under a steeply pitched slate roof. Seating was provided for 150 people with the traditional wooden bench seat combined with a kneeler for the row behind. These were set on either side of a central aisle. There was only one main altar at the end with the red sentry light hanging from the ceiling directly in front.

Five sets of gothic arched windows provided the natural light down each side whilst a group of eight small round windows set around a larger window occupied the wall above the entrance that directly faced the altar. The usual adornments of the Stations of the Cross were set between the windows and statues of Mary and St Fidelis with their attendant racks of prayer candles flanked the entrance to the altar.

Jimmie in his best and neatly pressed BQMS uniform accompanied by his best man Bert, Nancy's brother, waited for his sweetheart in the front row on the right hand side. Behind him were his parents and three sisters. His to be in-laws arrived and seated themselves on the left, their presence telling him that Nancy was outside. The organ fanfare announced the arrival of the Bride in the church and on the arm of her father with Olive walking behind processed down the aisle until she stood beside her husband to be. This is the moment they had wanted, to make that union that they treasured and which was to remain steadfast through all the challenges that were to come until their deaths nearly 60 years later.

After the service, the confetti and photographs outside the church they returned to 239 Lower Road for the reception. Restricted by the time limit on his pass of 4 o'clock Monday morning and with only the Sunday service of public transport to get him back there was to be no honeymoon only a few hours to enjoy together. Many months were to pass before he saw his bride again.

The phoney war was to continue with further drops of letters to the German People but on the 18th December it got very serious for the RAF and the reality of war was brought home to our bomber crews and their families.

Intelligence was received that some of the German Fleet had left their dockyard. A daylight raid, the infamous Heligoland Bight raid was organised for the 18th December

1939. It involved 22 Wellington bombers. One of those aircraft that took part belonged to 149 Squadron based at RAF Mildenhall and was allocated the squadron code letter R for Robert. When they arrived at the target they discovered that the enemy had returned to port and was therefore by the rules of engagement, at the time, not deemed to be a target. The aircraft still heavy with their bombs turned for home and became part of a turkey shoot for the German fighters. R for Robert was one of the ten that returned to fly another day albeit only until 31st December 1940 when it sunk beneath the waters of Loch Ness where it remained until discovered in September 1985.

On 10th May 1940 the Germans attacked through Belgium and the Phoney War suddenly changed to a killing war. Appeasement stopped in the UK with the resignation of Chamberlain and the appointment of Churchill. Churchill's start was unfortunate insomuch that it coincided with what was nearly the annihilation of the Allied armies in France. However, a brilliant strategic move called Operation Dynamo turned defeat into victory as "we fought them on the beaches" and evacuated Dunkirk. By the 4th of June we had to survive as an island nation, to regroup and rebuild ready to return in the future.

In the meantime back on Epsom Downs Jimmie settled into the routine of military life. The day started with Reveille, a scramble to get washed and shaved, then breakfast. Next were gun drills, maintenance and driving instruction as well as individual training. The process of toughening up included PT, long route marches and cross-country running. Jimmie struggled with his cross-country, he was told it would get better when he got his second wind, but he never did. Practice trench digging was one way that time could be spent. There were trenches dug outside of Epsom towards Chessington another by the Drift Bridge near Banstead. The big advantage of digging near the Drift Bridge was the closeness of the pub by the same name. On occasions exercises were combined for example on one day they would route march to Richmond Park a mere ten miles away. Whilst there they would then practice 'cover from view' which involved lying down in the long grass for a chat or a smoke before the ten mile return journey.

By November he reached another landmark in his personal ambition to make his father proud of him. On the 23rd he attained the same rank in the same battalion and the same company as his father had 25 years earlier. He was appointed Warrant Officer Third Class, so apart from the date the Warrants would be identical. Although it wasn't a case of déjà vu it certainly felt like it, as has happened so many times in his life that he thought history was repeating itself.

The long nights of winter shortened with the oncoming of springtime. During this time Jimmie was demonstrating his abilities to learn, instruct and command. As well as all this he even managed to get a few days leave, which he spent relaxing at Belvedere. His end of training report (Army Form B2091) in May showed that he was a good instructor in the Bren gun, Vickers machine gun and the Boys anti-tank rifle. As well as being a keen and smartly turned out Warrant Officer his report also said that he had a "good standard of intelligence and was of sound character" and "has proved to be a good sound TSM". The special notes written by his Commanding Officer was complimentary of his general abilities and conduct. He was convinced there was officer material in the young Knox and recommended him for officer cadet training.

On 9th May 1940 he packed his kit bag and boarded a train headed for Kent. He alighted at what is now Folkestone West Station, in 1940 there were no signs but it was simply known as "Shorncliffe Camp". From the station Jimmie set out on the 2 mile walk to the camp. On arrival at the Sir John Moore barracks he reported for duty at the Officer Cadet Training Unit.

Shorncliffe Camp is near Folkestone in Kent and was originally built as a Napoleonic earthworks fort in 1794. Sir John Moore, after whom the barracks were named, was placed in charge of the coastal defences from Dover to Dungeness. At the time it was thought that a previous warlord, Napoleon, had his eyes set on invading England. On his initiative the military canal in Kent and Sussex was cut and its now quiet and peaceful waters still flow through Folkestone their military necessity lost to history. To fortify the coast he also built a series of Martello Towers. Each tower spaced such that they could give covering fire to each other. They were modelled on the towers that had he had seen offer stout resistance to the British sea and land forces at Mortella Point in Corsica. During his time at Shorncliffe in 1803 Sir John Moore established an innovative training regime that produced Britain's first permanent light infantry regiments and its tradition was what Jimmie was now to experience.

When Jimmie arrived the camp was still coming to terms with the greater intake of trainees caused by the onset of war. The promised new accommodation huts were not ready, so the single story brick huts last used as officers quarters in 1923 were used as temporary accommodation. The ivy was pulled off the walls and the shutters opened and that was it. The only luxury was the marble topped washstands last used by officers. The newspapers managed to spin this by claiming that because their accommodation was not ready the new intakes were temporarily housed in the luxury of the Officer's Mess.

He was taken on the strength as a cadet in the 163rd. designated as The Artists Rifles where he joined many others from the London area. Most Regiments in the British Army are proud of their long history of achievements and traditions and the Artists Rifles was not to be outdone on this score. Its history dated back to its formation in 1859 as a volunteer force in response to the threatened invasion by Napoleon. The group was organised by Edward Sterling who was an art student and he tried to only attract various professional painters, musicians, actors, architects and others involved in creative endeavours; a profile he strove to maintain for some years. The Artists Rifles had Battle Honours in the Second Boer War and France in 1917 and 1918. It became difficult to recruit to its original intentions and the regiment gradually broadened its intake to include professions rather than purely artistic ones. The Artists Rifles became so popular that recruitment was eventually restricted to a recommendation from existing members of the battalion. Because of its specialised recruitment procedures during the First World War it became a specialised officer training unit. Many of the officers that passed through accruing a large number of decorations including 8 Victoria Crosses and fifty-six DSOs in the First World War. The regiment was not deployed during the Second World War it was purely used for officer training throughout the period. (Since then it has gone on to produce many fine SAS officers.) It was into these elite that Jimmie proudly signed on as an Officer Cadet in May 1940.

For the next four months there was little time for relaxation. In the words of Sir Arthur Bryant, the historian, "Sir John Moore's contribution to the British Army was not only the matchless Light Infantry, who have ever since enshrined his training, but also the belief that the perfect soldier can only be made by evoking all that is finest in man - physical, mental and spiritual". With this in mind the instructors at the OCTU put Jimmie's character and ability under the spotlight.

His Company Commander's report at the end of the month read.

> *"A very good type, His knowledge is above the average. He was inclined to be very proud of the fact he knew a good deal more than the others. He has improved considerably".*

He continued training endeavouring to take on board criticism and to further develop his character; to be able to control himself both in words and actions especially as the pressure was applied over the coming months. To misquote Rudyard Kipling "If you can keep your head when all about you are losing theirs then you are an Officer my son."

He started to excel in his ability to command. The next month's report read

> *"Doing very well indeed, and shows power of command and outstanding ability generally. Should do very well".*

By hard work, enthusiasm and application he succeeded as a good and capable cadet with an excellent ability to command. His final report by his Company Commander was perhaps a good summary of his character and ability.

> *"Has proved himself an outstanding cadet. His power of command is excellent and when his ways have "fined down" and experience in the infantry gained, he should go far."*

Although he "fined down" Jimmie never really changed; he always carried himself proudly perhaps giving the impression of a slight tint of superiority.

His commanding Officer complemented this report by his comments writing

> *"A very good and capable cadet.*
> *Outstanding from point of view of ability.*
> *Should do very well and make a first rate officer."*

With a final complimentary comment on his record that his

> *"Military conduct was very good"*

he was discharged from OCTU at the end of August under Para 383 having been appointed a commission.

Later in his life Jimmie still remained proud of what he had achieved at OCTU as he said, "In those days the two things essential to become an officer were Cert A and a bank account neither of which I had", so understandably he must, at that time, have been ebullient over his achievement and deservedly so.

R&R at Belvedere

Chapter 4   From "N" & "I" to "NI"

A year of the war had already passed and as yet Jimmie had not fired a shot in anger. He had watched as others fought and died in the skies as the RAF took on the might of the Luftwaffe in the months of the Battle of Britain. The closest he had been to danger was when returning German bombers who failed to reach their target decided to deliver their lethal load on another target as a farewell present before they left the shores of England. Folkestone was targeted partially because of the harbour and Shorncliffe Camp. The gasworks and railway also received attention together with the nearby airfield at Hawkinge. In this way as Folkestone was one of the last vestiges of England before the Channel and safety the area received its share of the blitz.

Having been kicked out of France and with the Nazis commanding most of the countries facing Britain it became essential that the Kriegsmarine German was not allowed to roam free and wide. To bring their fleet from their home ports at Bremen, Wilhelmshaven, Kiel, and Hamburg they would have to run the gauntlet down the English Channel or they would have to use the North Sea and loop over the top of the Shetland Islands. They could then use the deep channel between the Faroe Islands and Iceland to make good their escape into the Atlantic. Both the German and British high Command appreciated this and Germany had been making overtures to Iceland which alarmed the UK Government. The UK Government was also aware that the neutral waters of Norway were enabling Germany to transport Swedish iron ore to their factories in the Ruhr. The Germans had made various violations of these neutral waters before they invaded Norway at the beginning of April 1940. The UK's response was to send two Brigades of the 49th (West Riding) Infantry Division to Norway. The 49th Division was composed mainly of part-time soldiers. In addition to being almost completely green and inexperienced, they had received very little appropriate training for the operation they were to undertake, which in comparison to the Germans left them at a great disadvantage. They were an ill-prepared force on an ill-prepared mission to try and save Norway. They were expected to inhibit the use of Norwegian ports for Germany's commercial transportation of Swedish iron ore and for their use by the German Navy as it leapfrogged along the Norwegian coast to get out into the Atlantic.

To support the Norwegian Army defending Trondheim the 146th Brigade under the Mauriceforce landed at Namos in the central north of Norway between 14th-18th April and after a lot of heavy fighting and bad luck were evacuated two weeks later on 2nd May.

At the same time, 400 Km to the south the 148th infantry brigade, which incorporated 1/5th Battalion of the Leicester's, under Sickleforce landed at Åndalsnes in Romsdal, between 17th-19th April. They were then diverted to take on the Germans coming out of Oslo. They managed to advance 270 Km to Lillehammer before being driven back. In the fighting they suffered over 60% casualties and many taken prisoner before eventually withdrawing. The remnants of the 148th, 300 men and nine officers, were evacuated on 1st May and returned to the UK with the Leicesters going to Northern Ireland. The Brigade never again recovered as a fighting unit. Although they could claim to be the first territorial troops to fight in the war it must have been one of the shortest and unsuccessful campaigns of the Second World War.

With the battle for Norway lost and the threat of the Kriegsmarine being able to escape into the Atlantic with the dismal effect that would have on the UK's survival the new Bulldog in No 10 Downing Street ensured that Britain took matters into their own hands. On the 10th May 1940, disregarding Iceland's declared neutrality Britain invaded. It was a short swift and painless victory enabling a British base to be established in the harbour of Reykjavík. Meeting no resistance, the troops moved quickly to disable communication networks, secure strategic locations, and arrest German citizens. Requisitioning local transport, the troops moved to Hvalfjörður, Kaldaðarnes, Sandskeið, and Akranes thus securing areas of potential advantage to the Germans if they attacked.

Iceland was then used as a British base for the aircraft and naval vessels able to patrol the northern waters that could be used as the escape route for the Kriegsmarine. In later years they assisted in the protection of the Russian Convoys to Murmansk. To provide the necessary military presence for the defence and running of the various strategic bases on the island the 49th (West Riding) Infantry Division was called upon. 146th Brigade after its trauma of Norway was sent there together with 147th Brigade that as yet had not seen action as it did not receive the call to go to Norway. To the bulk of the troops in 146th bde and 147th bde Iceland was just a place they had seen on a map and because it wasn't coloured Empire pink it would have been given scant attention in their elementary education. They would have assumed because of its geographical position just outside the Arctic Circle it would be rather like its name suggested. So you can imagine their surprise when they arrived in what was to be a record warm temperature of 24^0C, with snow capped mountains in the distance it seemed like an idyllic place. With all the work that needed to be done to build defensive positions and anti-aircraft emplacements around the docks and airfield they soon managed to work up a sweat. After a bit of a frosty reception to start with from the Islanders they soon became friendly and invited the soldiers to share in their warm thermal springs. Some of the local girls became even friendlier leading to several complaints being made to the town's mayor about houses of ill repute and prostitution, however, in the end common sense prevailed when it was realised that what was happening was between consenting adults.

At first it seemed strange that there was no real night time but then the days started to shorten and the temperature started to drop. By October the temperature had dropped to that of a British mid-winter and the necessary patrols had ceased to be enjoyable. As time went on the days shortened even more. The temperature kept moving down remaining in the negative region all day and going down towards double negative figures at night that in turn dragged the day temperatures further down. The rain turned to snow and the snow settled and got thicker and thicker. With the summer gone and although the war seemed far away the gilt was coming off the gingerbread. It was no fun patrolling in the winter weather. As they moved about outside their khaki uniforms soon got covered in snow and as a sailor remarked to one snow covered patrol "You look more like bloody Polar Bears than soldiers".

This comment went back into camp at the patrol's end and evoked the general feeling that's exactly what they thought they were at times.

"If that's what we are why don't we change our insignia to Polar Bear?"

There was a general consensus that this was a good idea so they approached the CO. He, in turn, agreed to change the insignia if a suitable emblem was submitted.

That started a competition to produce a new insignia using a Polar Bear. There were several suggestions, some not too serious. In the end it was decided to have a Polar Bear standing on a small ice flow with his head down in its natural attack stance. It was approved by the CO on 29th July '41 and the order went out that the insignia of the current white rose of York was to be replaced by the Polar Bear and the new insignia went into service on 1st September that year. Those entitled to wear it would have included the 148th in Northern Ireland 900 miles to the south.

The psychological effect of the defeat in Norway was to be shielded from the rest of the troops in the UK so the broken and demoralised 148th were taken to Belfast and then southwards to a small village called Caledon just inside the border of the county of Tyrone with Co Armagh. Troublesome Co Monaghan in the Irish Free State of Southern Ireland was under 3 Km away.

As far back as 1542 when Henry VIII declared that the English controlled the Kingdom of Ireland there has been simmering if not open opposition by some elements of the Irish. It has been a split within the island of Ireland mainly along religious grounds perhaps promoted by the Papal support for the Protestant William of Orange instead of the catholic maternal uncle of James II. However, in 1693 another Pope recognised James as the continuing King of Great Britain and Ireland. Sectarianism broke out with the Anglicans forming the Orange Order opposed by the Catholic Defenders both founded in the County of Armagh on the boundary of which sits Caledon. There have been many attempts to find a solution to the "Irish problem". In 1801 Ireland was included in the new state of the United Kingdom of Great Britain and Ireland and the red diagonal cross of St Patrick was added to the UK flag making it the one we recognise today. Unfortunately this did not end the mixed feelings in Ireland and ended up with the Irish War of Independence. A deal to try and broker peace was entered into in 1921 where Ireland was partitioned each part with its own government but continued to remain part of the UK. This fell apart fairly rapidly with the Catholic southern and western states forming the Irish Free State.

It was into this fractionalised country that the 148th arrived. What was unknown to them, or anybody else, at the time was that the British government had tried to get the

Southern States to join with the allies against fascist Germany on the promise of a united and independent Ireland. The Irish Taoiseach Eamon de Valera in his wisdom had decided that Churchill could not deliver on the promise and thus decided that Southern Ireland would remain a neutral region. This put Churchill's back up and he did not hesitate to place an embargo on all goods that flowed across the border.

During their arrival briefing they were told about the ultimatum sent to the Foreign Secretary Lord Halifax on 12th December 1939 by Patrick Flemming issued on behalf of the Irish Republican Army (IRA) Council. The communiqué informed them of

> *"...the Government of the Irish Republic's intention to go to war against Great Britain"*

although they did provide a caveat that there would be no actions taken against the Northern States. The Leicesters were there to patrol the border to stop any IRA activities especially gun-running.

Caledon was not really ready for the arrival of so many troops. It was life under canvas until more permanent Nissan huts were constructed at the north end of the village in the fields between the town and the Churchyard off John's Hill Road. The officers, however, managed to find accommodation at Caledon Castle or with local farmers. In the main, life was not too dangerous. Unfortunately just before Second Lieutenant Knox arrived there had been a fatality involving a lorry full of troops heading north out of Caledon. The roads and lanes around the village were narrow and poorly surfaced. Drainage was achieved by ditches running alongside the road. On 12th August 1940, the month before he arrived, a lorry with a group of troops in the back was slowly climbing the hill out of Caledon. It had turned onto a narrow lane called Minterburn Road and was struggling to get to 20 mph when two small children appeared just in front of the lorry. The surprised lorry driver, Private R.H.Walls, swerved to avoid them causing the lorry to leave the road and head for the nearby field situated on the other side of a drainage ditch. Unfortunately, the driver was unable to control the vehicle. The front wheel dug into the drainage ditch and the rear of the vehicle reared upwards and over, on the way it jettisoned the soldiers in the back injuring eight of them. All but one, Lance Sergeant Thomas Radford, was thrown clear. Radford ended up being trapped under the lorry suffering several broken ribs. Regrettably, before they could release him he suffocated. This was a black day for the Leicesters as it was the first incident where they had lost a fellow soldier whilst serving in Ireland.

When Radford's parents heard the news they requested that their son, who was only 21 when he died, was returned to be buried in Leicester's Belgrade Cemetery close to where they lived. The request was granted and the return of Radford became one of the first things that Jimmie was made aware of on his arrival.

Jimmie arrived in Caledon on Friday 6th September 1940 a warmer than usual late summer's day with the welcoming sun shining from a clear blue sky. He reported to Alexander House situated half way up Main Street. It was a grey stone building with thick walls and small windows with two stout wooden doors opening via a short flight of stone steps directly onto the pavement. After a brief welcome by his CO he was introduced to one of his fellow officers a nineteen year old Second Lieutenant Mansel-Pleydell, whose mother was a Countess and whose father Ralf had served in the First World War. Fortunately, to his fellow officers he was just called John.

John took him to Caledon Castle the home of Eric James Desmond Alexander, 5th Earl of Caledon. Jimmie was going to be temporarily billeted there in the converted stable block until he could organise himself lodgings with one of the local farmers. The Castle as it was called was a fine stone-built house originally built in 1779 by the current incumbent's great grandfather. Over time it had been extended to three stories. The garden frontage had one bay on either side of a broad, central, curved bow. The rear elevation displayed a wide spread of eight pairs of Ionic columns supporting a first floor veranda that stretched across the whole width of the main building and the two wings. Above was a high centrally placed pediment on which was boldly placed the Caledon Arms. The castle was set in 3000 acres of woodland to the southwest of the village, bordered on the eastern and southern sides by the River Blackwater and extended over the border into Co Monaghan, now one of the Free Irish States. The castle itself benefitted from the services of the troops who helped out during their spare time to keep the grounds in good order.

When given his appointment at Shorncliffe Jimmie was told that part of his duties was to improve the morale of the troops after their drumming in Norway. This was also confirmed by his CO as part of his welcoming brief. It was at his first parade that he began to appreciate the level to which the moral had sunk. Whilst there was an attempt to be smart on parade there were clear indications as to why morale was bad. Yes their uniforms were clean but the webbing was First World War vintage and so were their bayonets. He felt that if he could get them the correct uniform they would feel smart and psychologically it would be a step in the right direction. When it came to the practical side of soldiering it was obvious that they lacked basic training. The only thing they had going for them was that they had been bloodied in battle although, given the number of their colleagues that had been killed and wounded he was unsure if it really was a plus or not.

With his experience of training in a wide range of weapons Jimmie soon set up some training and practical use of the rifle, Bren and general machine gun. As with his previous experience with training the use of his analogy of a slice of cake with the field of fire from a machine gun enabled the troops to understand its power and limitations. The shooting range was in a field close to St John's Church and backed downhill onto the River Blackwater. The river and its often used flood plain area provided a natural backstop to the ammunition that went in its general direction. After assembling at the camp for those on shooting practice it was a sharp right wheel onto Church Hill Road, A march past the graveyard and then the church before another right wheel into the field. Improvements in fieldcraft and tactics were carried out in a large open country area including woodlands near a place called Kilsampson on the west side of the village. To get to this area it involved a sharp left wheel outside the camp and along Main Street before turning into Killylea Road. It was a march of 1 Km and was often taken at the double.

The training was proceeding well; the morale was now on the rise. As the troop's stamina and abilities were improved local competitions were organised with the Wiltshire's and Lord Caledon's home guard. This all helped to improve their morale. Pride in themselves and their unit had returned and they were once again living up to their nickname of the "Tigers". They were soon anxious to get back into the fight to show the Germans what was what. Unfortunately this was never to be and they spent the rest of the war serving on the home front in Northern Ireland. They sadly watched in 1942 the Americans and Belgium's use the locality to train their troops for operation Overlord knowing they were not to join them.

The depredations on the other side of the border were beginning to bite. They had noticed on their patrols that the number of cars on the southern roads had all but vanished as the supply, or rather lack, of petrol had dried up. Cars were replaced by bicycles or a farmer may use a horse and cart. Unemployment was on the increase as their economy spiralled downwards. The shortage of domestic goods, normally supplied from the north, forced up prices. The twin effects of unemployment with its loss of earnings and the increase in prices brought about in the first instance an increase in crime. This was followed by a decline in living standards and the subsequent decline in public health. The area on the south side of the border was slowly slipping back in time and before too long to go south was like travelling back in time some 700 years.

For the troops and police along the border that formed a line with a neutral country smuggling and its associated black market became a big problem. Not everything was one-sided as there were shortages on the northern side of the border just like the rest of Britain they were suffering from shortages caused by the war. So there was many a time when a skinny girl would travel across the border only to return days later heavily pregnant. This happened in both directions and no doubt a Nelson's eye would have been turned to some of the trafficking. The national drink in Ireland is the black stuff brewed in Dublin and it became in high demand in the north leading to it being considered as an economic weapon by the Irish. Locally no doubt even Nelson's good eye would not have noticed the flow of the black stuff to the town's bars.

With the open threat by the IRA of attacks against the British mainland special attention had to be paid to gunrunning as well as bomb making materials crossing the border. There must have been occasions when hot-blooded border pursuits were made and it is possible that on Sunday 17th November during one of these occasions that it fell ill for his fellow officer John Mansel-Pleydell. Regrettably he was killed, it happened just five days before his twentieth birthday. John being a Roman Catholic was buried in the churchyard at the Catholic Church at Aughnacloy on the Minterburn Road to the north of Caledon.

His grave carries the inscription

John Aymard Morton Mansel-Pleydell
108163
2nd Lieutenant Leicesters

Eternal rest give unto him O Lord
and
let perpetual light shine upon him Amen.

It was during this time that Jimmie managed to get lodgings with a local farmer and then managed to get permission to bring his wife away from the London Blitz to join him in Caledon. With some leave due he went to Belvedere and returned to Caledon with Nancy. She loved it in Caledon and the two agreed that they could easily live there. She got on well with the young couple running the farm, joining in the milking and collecting the eggs. She and Jimmie would walk the lanes together and talk to the Parrot in a roadside cage at a nearby junction. Nancy's only concern and it was a serious concern was that the farm owners were very staunch Unionists and she feared for her life. Had they known that seven years ago at the age of sixteen she converted to the Roman Catholic Faith she was convinced that no matter how welcoming they were they would not have hesitated to slit her throat one night. Fortunately this never came to pass and the two enjoyed their time together, the only real time that they had been able to spend since they had married in September 1939.

During late July and early August there were rumours about some changes to the Army. There was talk of new Regiments or Corps being formed. This was all the result of the initial report from a committee set up to investigate the reasons for the recent failures and to make proposals for the future. Slowly the talk took on a more substantial form. It was said that one of the reasons for the recent failures was because the infantry did not have accurate and up to date information about the disposition of the enemy's troops. Most of the information gathered in the past had been achieved because individual sections had sent out their own scouts to try and establish the enemy's strength and disposition. Unfortunately there was no constructive or set pattern to acquiring this information so what was discovered was sketchy, or late in arriving or both. In the preparations for the anticipated invasion of the UK mainland defence exercises had been carried out. During these exercises a number of infantry battalions had formed Recce platoons using motorcycle riders to provide a quick method of feeding the information back to HQ. In exercises this had proved hugely successful. To some extent Jimmie's patrols of the border country with Southern Ireland had already introduced him to this type of reconnaissance and he enjoyed the thought of action and adrenalin rush of reconnaissance.

Jimmie & Nancy at Caledon 1940

Chapter 5   Reconnaissance Corps

The second quarter of 1940 was a disaster militarily. Chased out of Norway at the end of May; Driven out of France at Dunkirk in June under operation Dynamo; Evacuations from the Cherbourg Peninsular under operation Cycle in July and finally from the Atlantic coast of France under operation Aerial. Although operationally these were military defeats they soon became heralded as victories for saving in total 450,000 of our armed services as well as numbers of French, Belgium, Polish and Canadian soldiers.

It was the fast moving Blitz Krieg of the German Army that had effectively caught out the British Army and clearly indicated to them and Churchill in particular that this war was not going to be anything like the static trench warfare of the First World War. Churchill quickly established a committee to investigate the reasons for this trouncing and to put forward a proposal for changes that could be made quickly in the face of the threat of invasion. To chair this committee Churchill appointed Sir George Bartholomew, recently retired as General Officer Commanding Northern Command.

The Bartholomew Committee, as it became known, was quick off the mark and had a draft proposal ready in July when a proposal to change some of the old school practices was made. This was watered down as the draft passed through the Army's bureaucracy. It was again compromised because of the loss of major quantities of materials and armaments during the evacuations from France, so ultimately very little was adopted. The main fear of an immediate invasion effectively stopped the proposals for a redesign of the heavy weaponry as the existing production facilities were prioritised for the continuation in the manufacturing of existing weapons.

The main change that was accepted and went forward was the appreciation that in a fast moving front it was essential that the infantry and guns knew where the enemy was positioned and its strength. The system currently used to achieve this by the infantry was to use its troops to reconnoitre. It was done on an ad hoc arrangement using motorcyclists and light tanks but there was no truly constructed approach and the information gained was only of use to the local commander.

So it was no flight of fancy that lay behind the formation of the Reconnaissance Corps. Its birth was the result of practical thinking and detailed analysis by the Bartholomew Committee. On 16th September 1940 the decision was taken that the infantry was to be the providers for this new force although, they would in 1944 become part of the Royal Armoured Corps. One of the consequences of incorporation under the RAC banner was the changing of familiar infantry terminology to that of the cavalry. It all happened in June 1942 when a Brigade became a Regiment, Companies became Squadrons and Platoons became Troops. The black beret of the RAC was also adopted and a new regimental colouring of gold and green braid on officer's tunics. The number 41 on a green over gold diagonally split background as identification for their vehicles was also introduced. A new badge was forthcoming depicting a central spear indicating attack with a lightning flash on either side indicating the speed of the attack.

Whilst the main use of the Recce was to find and probe the enemy's positions, to exploit the weak spots driving a bridgehead through enabling more troops to follow. It was also used as a radio communications link from forward positions to guns. It would gather information about the activities and resources of the enemy, or about the natural features and other activities in the area through which the army would have to pass. This meant that they were usually operating forward of their own lines and this lead to their motto. "Only the enemy in front", which Richard

Doherty used as a title for his book adding the equally true subheading "every other bugger behind".

It was obvious that speed and good communications were an essential part of the Recce and secondly they would also have to be capable of defending themselves should they run into problems. This new type of scout or cavalry needed special means of transport. It had to be fast, manoeuvrable, armoured and packed with a punch. There was not going to be a single panacea vehicle. The result of a lot of work in a very demanding time scale was a number of armoured vehicles, some more successful than others. The armoured car was born. It came in various types or styles. The 'light' was a fast but lightly armoured and weaponed vehicle and a 'heavy' whose armour could take more punishment whilst its punch was designed to cope with all but the big tanks. There was also a third vehicle that was added to the complement. Whereas the armoured cars were wheeled vehicles this third vehicle was tracked. It became known as the Universal Carrier, or sometimes it was called the Bren Carrier because of its light armaments of a Bren light machinegun. It was envied by the Germans because it was very flexible in its use. It could become a troop carrier, mobile mortar platform or equipment transporter either directly or by towing. Because of its tracks it could go a lot of places wheeled vehicles and heavy armour couldn't. It was only limited in its abilities by the imagination of its users, hence the name Universal. It ended up being so popular that over 52,000 were produced, twice that of the number of armoured cars. There was also the combo vehicle, the half-track with one of its uses being able to quickly deposit the assault troops. Jimmie would be introduced to all of these and more when he went on his Armoured Fighting Vehicle course at the end of 1942.

Chapter 6   Learning to Lead Out Front

There was discussion about the new regiment, if that was what it was to be, and how it was to be formed. Its duty was clear it was to be reconnaissance. Because it was a force needed by the infantry it would be under their jurisdiction. But then they were to be a fast-moving force with armoured cars so they were really a cavalry unit which would come under the Royal Armoured Corps. As far as Jimmie was concerned he didn't particularly worry about how it was controlled, however, he did like the sound of this new concept. He realised that if they were introducing or recruiting a new Reconnaissance unit then one of them must be for the 148th Brigade since they currently did not have one. Thus when the opportunity happened, he took the decision that formulated the rest of his army career and volunteered for the Recce. His request was granted and he was initially transferred on 13th December to the 148th Anti-tank. His Majesty King George VI on the 14th January 1941 signed a Royal Warrant "to authorise the formation of a corps to be entitled Reconnaissance Corps" and so it was that the 148th Anti-tank became the 148th Recce Corps, and subsequently Jimmie went to a war he might otherwise have missed.

Reporting to the 148th meant a change from Caledon away from a more relaxed life and the advantages of having his wife with him. The couple had made their farewells to the farm and bid the Leicesters *bon chance,* he took Nancy home. He returned to Northern Ireland across the 32 miles of the Irish Sea from Cairnryan in Scotland to Larne, a trip which in those days would take two and a half hours. Three miles to the west of the port of Larne was his new base in Castle Kilwaughter.

He was now based in County Antrim, one of the six counties that formed the new region of Northern Ireland; it is located in the northeast corner of Ireland straddling the land between the Irish Sea and Lough Neagh. The Irish Sea forms its border on the north-west with County Down on the south and Londonderry on the west. Lough Neagh was the central hub for five of the six counties with Fermanagh being the loner.

Kilwaughter Castle set in gently rolling hills was originally built in the early 19th Century for the Agnew family. At the outbreak of war, ownership had passed to the Balzani family. Il Duce did the Balzani family no favours when he went under the Axis banner. Since the Balzanies were an Italian family this enabled the British Government to declare the property as being on enemy territory and so it was taken over by the Ministry of defence. Initially used as a base for the 148th Recce Corp until 1944 when they were replaced by the American 644th Tank Destroyer Battalion. The countryside in this part of Ireland was ideal with its rolling hills and small country lanes providing experiences similar to that they would encounter in Northern Europe. The flat land on the coast at Mulligan, Co Derry provided shooting practice and the coast around Lough Neagh near Antrim enabled experience at defending from and making amphibious landings to be gained.

There was a lot to learn. One of the main differences that became obvious to him was the general level of intelligence and IQ of not only his fellow officers but also that of the rank and file. Changes were constantly being made as the Recce began to improve and consolidate how it was to function not only as a Corp but also in relation to those that needed its services.

He now had to learn how to drive an armoured car and be able to put it through its paces learning its advantages as well as its limitations. Communications were critical after all there is no point sending a patrol out to find the enemy if they can't tell anybody what they have found and more than that exactly where they are so the artillery can come to bear accurately. Flags, hand signals and the Aldis lamp were part of the basic training but were of little use in battlefield conditions. Thus knowledge in the use and maintenance of the 1938 designed single channel No 11 radio transceiver had to be gained. Whilst it was an improvement over the No 1 set it was limited in speech range to six miles and double that when using Morse Code, which fortunately Jimmie had already learnt.

Jimmie and his colleagues were proficient in Morse and they used it to their advantage. When out at the local they found that they could discuss the local girls by tapping on the table. Jimmie in those days was a pipe smoker and was proficient at clicking the stem between his teeth.

"dit dit dit dit dit dit   dit/ dit dit dit dit dit / dah dah dah dah dit dah".

The No 19 set was the next generation that came into service in 1940/41. It was an improvement as it was a three channel transceiver enabling the A set to communicate long range with the squadron or regiment HQ and the B set for inter troop short range communications. The IC set was used for internal crew communication. With the driver and gunner only connected to the IC. In normal use the three channels were mixed onto the IC so that all the crew could monitor the radio calls. The commander or operator could then select the A or B sets and remove them from the IC and allow push-to-talk. A warning lamp would light if one set was left unmonitored. Later control boxes allowed the commander or operator to rebroadcast A onto B or vice versa for message relay. The driver's control box incorporated a push button to activate a buzzer, allowing the commander's attention to be brought back to the IC if a situation requiring his attention arose. So as the No 19 sets were installed there was another learning curve where plenty of practice was required.

1941 soon passed and with the Japanese attack on Pearl harbour on the 7th December the American Congress declared war on The Empire of Japan the following day. On the 11th December Hitler took one of his most puzzling decisions when he declared war on the USA. Once again the American response was immediate and the might of the great American war machine became engaged directly in the war in Europe. The tide of the war was about to change. It was obvious not only to the military but also the man in the street that a return to mainland Europe had to be a first step in defeating Hitler. This was not going to happen overnight. The military thinking had to adjust itself from the defence of Britain to attack and that would mean that fortress Britain would have to make itself the holder of all the troops and weaponry necessary to make it happen. More to learn for Jimmie and the Recce and more places to go in preparation for the upcoming big push.

With the change in footing, the military life in the Corps got very hectic and more time was being spent away from their base camp. Jimmie managed to get some Christmas leave having to return to Kilwaughter Castle to make ready for a move on the 18th January. The move was across Co Antrim to the capital town on the banks of Lough Neagh. Their base was the impressive building of Antrim Castle. It was a journey of twenty miles and having departed by 10.00 hours they were all in by 16.30 hours. There is little clue in their War Diary as to the purpose of the move. One can only speculate that it gave them practice at different harbour layouts as well as the ability to practice defence from the water attacks.

On the 3rd of February they were on the move again. This time it was fifty-five miles to the north into Co Derry and the practice firing ranges at Magilligan. A suitably chosen flat and desolate area surrounded on three sides by water. After spending three days practising with live ammunition they repacked their vehicles on 7th February and returned the sixty-four miles to Kilwaughter and back to where they started.

On the 1st March Jimmie and another of his fellow junior officers, Castle, were promoted to War Substantive rank of Lieutenant. After a short handover period of only two days Lieutenant Worrall left to attend a course at the Recce Junior Leaders School situated at Annan in Dumfriesshire in South West Scotland. The following week on 12th March he was followed by Sergeant Ings and the week after that on the 18th by Captain Dixon who after completing the course on 4th April was posted to 146th Brigade headquarters in Iceland.

On the 23rd March it was bags packed again for another sixty-four-mile convoy to Magilligan this time for advanced training only to pack their bags again for the return trip five days later.

The build-up for the invasion was underway. Foreign troops, mostly American began to be positioned all over Northern Ireland as well as on the mainland. On the 11th of April an order was received instructing them to prepare for a move to Uttoxeter on the mainland. On the 25th of April they moved out of Kilwaughter Castle to a holding camp at Larne. The following day they embarked for the two and a half hour, thirty-two mile crossing to Cairnryan in Stranraer. The crossing was made without incident and after disembarking they divided into three parties. The first party of 142 travelled by train to their destination of the Poor Law Institute in Holly Road, Uttoxeter, Staffordshire. The second party to join them on the 27th was the carrier party that had travelled by train and last but not least on the 28th the third and final party, those with motor vehicles who had driven the 280 miles made it to the Poor Law Institute.

The Poor Law Institute in Uttoxeter was built in 1838/40 being one of a system of workhouses dotted about the country. It was popular during the First World War to use the old work, or poor, houses, for military use. Usually, because of the high injury rate, the more popular use in WW1 was as a hospital. In WW2 they were used mainly as barracks. Uttoxeter's building had been converted to a grammar school prior to the war; it was a single story building fronting the road with a central archway leading to a T-shaped main block. There was also a building that could be used as a medical centre as well as rooms for 200 people which should have been sufficient for 148th as they were only at Squadron strength.

On the 28th April T/Major A.G.P. Withington who had commanded them in Northern Ireland after having consolidated the squadron at Uttoxeter relinquished his command to T/Major J.H. Days of the Hampshire's with immediate effect.

They had no sooner got settled when on 8th May another warning order was received with instructions to prepare for another move this time the destination was unknown. There was obvious speculation as to the hidden agenda behind the move. Perhaps things are about to happen? To where were they going?

With Nancy now approaching the end of her second trimester, Jimmie managed to get nine days leave and on Friday 26th June he arrived in Belvedere. He was surprised at the amount of bomb damage that there was. Most of the houses on Abbey Road were no more than a pile of bricks as they had obviously been caught by a stick of bombs. Fortunately the area around Crabtree Manorway was unscathed. During his leave the sirens started their two-tone warning and all but Jimmie got up and gathering books and knitting left him behind as they headed for the cellar. Nancy called urgently to him to hurry up and join them in the cellar which they used as an air-raid shelter. No bombs were dropped and before long the single wail of the all-clear could be heard and life returned to normal.

On 4th July Belvedere Station was witness to another goodbye kiss as he bade her farewell and returned to camp to prepare for his deployment to the Junior Leaders School later that month. This was to be the last time that he was to see her before the arrival of their child. In those days the gender of the baby would remain a surprise until delivery and he would not know if he had a son or daughter until a letter or telephone call brought the news.

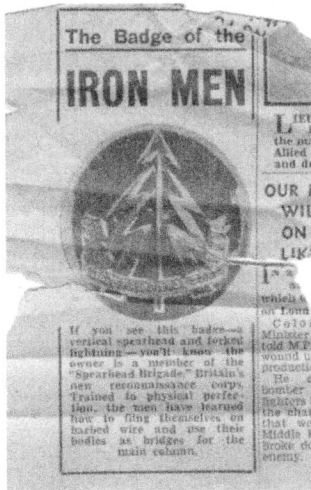

The Badge of the

IRON MEN

If you see this badge—a vertical spearhead and forked lightning—you'll know the owner is a member of the "Spearhead Brigade," Britain's new reconnaissance corps. Trained to physical perfection, the men have learned how to fling themselves on barbed wire and use their bodies as bridges for the main column.

Annan

Although the Army was still lagging a bit behind in its methodology on how the infantry was going to interact and employ the Recce in action it had by mid 1942 concluded the role and what was expected of the Recce. These new ideas were being taught to the new breed of intelligent officers attracted to the Recce in special training schools such as that at Annan in Dumfriesshire. It was at Annan that Jimmie had been allocated a place on the August Junior Leaders Course.

Annan sits in the south west of Scotland on the north side of the Solway Firth at its first fordable point. Historically this gave them advantages for trade but disadvantages in times of strife since it put them in the forefront of advancing troops. The town takes its name from the River Annan on which it stands 3Km from its mouth into the Solway Firth. The river was navigable for smaller ships as far as the road bridge in the town and by larger ships displacing 300 tons to a point 800 metres downstream from the town. The main buildings and structures in the town including the road bridge were made from locally quarried fine Triassic sandstone which appears a bit drab and grey on wet and overcast days but shows a deeper golden colour in the sun.

On 28th July kit bag and travel pass in hand, he was on the train to Annan. He was not the only one that was making his way to the Junior Leaders School and he was soon chatting to a couple of fellow officers. When the train arrived they alighted and crossed over the bridge to the down line platform where road access was available. With no military transport in sight they decided to share a taxi.

The course itself was fundamentally for NCOs and junior officers and it was not to be a walk in the park if the course was as tough as the entry requirements. All applicants applying to train at Annan had to pass an IQ test. It was essential to have the right calibre since in the field they would find themselves in situations where they would have to take responsibility for actions far above their rank. They needed to be intelligent, enterprising, brave, enduring and highly skilled. Their training was to include tactical deployment of not only sections and troops but also the whole squadron. They would study lessons learnt from recent operations, initially from the BEF in Normandy but later from Recce deployment in Egypt and Greece. This was achieved to some extent in the classroom where the technique of studying Tactical Exercises Without Troops or using its anachronism of TEWT was used. The idea was to break the group into small sections and pose them hypothetical scenarios. Given time for thought and consideration they had to put their solution to the trainers, who had heard most answers before and were able to give them a thoroughly hard time. The trainers would then give them their solution to the scenario following which it was expected and happened that the students would argue bringing forward various challenges. The whole purpose of the exercise was to get the junior officers to think laterally, to think outside the box, to see and seize opportunities both in attack and defence to their advantage.

They were introduced to the maxim that "Time spent in reconnaissance is seldom wasted" some thought that it should be "never wasted"

They would then go out into the surrounding countryside and imagine that they were on a search, find and report exercise. The instructors could at any moment pose a problem. On the first time out they would be posed the problem that the lead car had been taken out by a Panzerfaust antitank weapon. They would need to report the contact and the enemy's strength and composition together with their assessment of the situation. They would have to decide if it was an opportunity to exploit or not and if they needed support. Time pressure would now enter the situation and interesting arguments could develop as to the best solution. The questions that had to be answered included attack or withdrawal and how they would be achieved. Then consideration had to be given about the damaged vehicle and the occupants. When they thought they had that under control their situation was turned to place them in the damaged vehicle and how they would extract themselves.

On another time at a different location they were faced with finding a tank coming towards them. This presented them with a new set of circumstances. The enemy was now mobile but not necessarily fleet of foot and its armour would be strong enough to take being hit by the standard 2lb antitank weapon favoured by the British Army. The instructors could decide when, where and if one of the Recce's vehicles were hit. If they were, then how did the approach to the damaged vehicle change with a mobile enemy. Once again this was considered from the point of view of the remaining patrol vehicles as well as from the commander of the damaged vehicle's point of view.

Things would change again on the next outing. This time they would meet their opposite numbers, a German reconnaissance patrol. This gave the enemy greater tactical mobility with less protection so different proposals were sought, challenged and tested. Once again it was approached from both the patrol's point of view as well as the commander of a stricken vehicle's viewpoint. Time as always a constant source of pressure.

Consideration was also given to the use of the Recce in a defensive role. Because they were fleet of foot they could be used in rearguard actions as the main forces retired to a more favourable position. With the main troops re-established the Recce could fall back quickly and pass back through a line of greater defence suffering lower losses than a slower moving column.

Appreciation was also taught of the various speeds at which reconnaissance was conducted which depended on the surety of the enemy's position. A simple traffic light system was used. GREEN indicated that they were unlikely to meet opposition. Advances could be made directly towards their destination without the need to search the surrounding countryside. ORANGE was the first level of caution. This was where contact was likely so the speed of advance would be reduced with scout cars deviating off the direct route and searching the side roads. The slowest and most cautious approach would be RED when the enemy was known to be present. This called for close reconnaissance, usually this was undertaken on foot with armoured car support if things got tricky.

Sand table exercises were another source of presenting various scenarios and plenty of discussions regarding tactics. They would consider what they should think about if they came across a stream or river. Should they wait for support, could they cross the river and establish a bridgehead on the other side, holding the ground until support came and passed through? A bridge would pose another set of variables. Was it booby-trapped or under observation by an artillery group waiting for an attempted crossing? Of course it may not be the bridge that would be the target of any attack but the ground onto which the troops might deploy. Having studied and argued their cases on the sand table they could go into the countryside and look at conditions in the real world. Every possible situation was thrown at the trainees with the big reminder that there could always be a new one waiting in the field to confront them. All these were likely scenarios given the nature of the Recce's job and they needed an answer that was in time and correct. A second chance may not come their way!

Last but by no means least was to cover the school's thoughts on setting up camp at night or harbouring as it was known. Whilst this had been experienced by most of the pupils it was important to cover some salient points on the course. Not only had they to be undetectable from air or ground observation; any forward position that remains fixed for too long extends their discovery time with a resultant risk of accurate shelling or stonking as it was known.

Irrespective of tactics employed the one main objective of the Recce was to offensively probe the enemy front, find a weak spot, establish a bridgehead and allow more troops to pass through.

Not only did they have to have good knowledge of the vehicles used by the Allies but they also needed to know even more about the enemy. This would include being able to recognise the various types of vehicles that they used, their capabilities and their function. It was equally important to know the regimental unit markings and the epaulette colouring as these were used to denote operational functions and lastly but by no means least be aware of his tactics, to know and think like the enemy, to get inside his head.

As the course ended on 18th August Jimmie and his fellow students could clearly appreciate why the Recce demanded a very high standard from its officers. They were going to operate on their own initiative more than almost any others. Field and junior officers were to have responsibilities with few equals in any wartime army.

Introducing Porthcawl.

Porthcawl is a small coastal town situated in South Wales halfway between Cardiff and Swansea that enjoys a sea view of the Bristol Channel towards the North Devon coast. It was a well organised little town with its own ARP (Air Raid Precautions) as well as an efficient Home Guard section. The little harbour was home to a number of Air Sea Rescue launches. With representatives of the army and navy in the town the RAF was not to be left out. Four miles out of town on the A48 to Bridgend was a small RAF base called Stormy Down. It only had a grass runway with underlying subsidence problems, which put a restriction on the use of heavy aircraft at the base. The town had put in most precautions they could against bombing and attacks but little did they know until the end of the war that they would never be in the sights of a German bomber. Although they were not to suffer the impact of being bombed they were to witness the three consecutive night air raids on Swansea with the horizon glowing red a mere 22 Km across Swansea bay.

The town had its fair share of civilian evacuees and also welcomed a large variety of servicemen, especially on the build up to D-Day. They came from France, Holland, Canada, Poland and America as well as the British

Tommy of which Jimmie and his Regiment was to become one. It was Porthcawl that was the unknown destination that the 148th had received back on 8th May and it was to here that Jimmie returned after his spell at Annan. The arrival of the newly formed 148th Recce was all part of the planned build up for operation Overlord.

The 49th Division was earmarked as an assault division for the Normandy invasion and they were recalled from their stint in Iceland. Whilst in Iceland they had no requirement for a Reconnaissance unit but in view of their new prospective role, it became a necessity and into that role stepped the 148th Recce.

On 5th September 1942 The 49th Reconnaissance Regiment was formed in Porthcawl as part of the 49th (West Riding) Division from the 29th and 148th independent Reconnaissance Squadrons. They became "A" and "B" Squadrons together with the 1st Belgium Fusiliers that formed "C" Squadron. The diversity of the troops forming the 49th Recce gave them a confused identity as they had no particular association with Yorkshire other than by its name. In fact there were some that had previously worn the red rose on their shoulder. They were in many ways "Homeless" as they had nowhere to call their home town. As they had been formed at Porthcawl and some senior Officers had married local girls there began to be a strong association with the local area. Familiarity eased them into a situation where they were adopted, so to speak, by Porthcawl and it became their home town; the roots for which they had been searching.

Jimmie arrived back in Porthcawl on 19th August, just four weeks later on 16th September, the day before his third wedding anniversary he became a father for the first time; as far as he was aware he would jest when telling others. He managed to get nine days leave beginning on Friday the 2nd of October and Nancy knowing this had arranged for the Christening to be on Sunday the 4th. The weather was kind to them on that day with the sun shining giving a warm feel to that October Sunday. Both the families met again at Belvedere for the visit to St Fidelis Church, where the two had married only three years previously, for an afternoon christening service. The service was conducted by Father Charles Bellwood christening the next generation of the Knox clan as Peter Barry. He was named after Jimmie's best friend who unfortunately did not survive the war. Jimmie's sister Olive's husband Robert and Nancy's brother's wife Mary acted as God Parents. This was a big break with tradition since there had been three previous generations where the son had been called James Erskine. Jimmie said to Peter years later that he hoped that by not continuing the naming tradition he hadn't caused him to miss out on some great inheritance. (If it did Peter has not found out - yet.) The nine days of fussing over mother and baby rapidly flew past and Belvedere Station witnessed the final kisses and hugs for the new family of three people before he returned to South Wales. With little time to spare he organised his kit and made ready to leave for his next training session at the 49th Division Battle School in Birmingham.

Battle School

Before he left Porthcawl there was a certain amount of leg-pulling about how dangerous the battle schools were especially at Birmingham. If the Germans weren't going to get you with their bombing raids then the trainers and their helpers probably would. With these happy thoughts in mind Jimmy reported on 19th October.

The earlier comments he had received from his colleagues he put to the back of his mind as he reported for his first session. Then he found out the truth as he listened to the introduction.

"Since the debacle in Norway there has been a turnover in the division and there are a lot of you here today that may have fired a gun but have never been under fire. Over the next few days we are going to put that right. You are going on exercises which we will make as realistic to the real thing as possible. We will be shooting at you, throwing thunder flashes and dummy grenades. Although the machine guns will not be depressed to fire directly at you, they will be close. If you stick your arse in the air it might get another hole in it.

There are little things that should also concern you. In your training so far you have all experienced the bad rounds that kick up way off target or fall short. Here you will be on the receiving end of those rounds. Another little word that you might also like to contemplate is 'Ricochets'."

The concluding comment just in case anybody doubted the severity of the warning was "The Army expects to have causalities so nobody is going to kick my arse if any one or more, of you end up in hospital or worse!"

The battlefield inoculation began in no short measure. It was the noise that he found was the first big hurdle to overcome. To concentrate and communicate whilst being disorientated by the crack of the bullets just missing you and the thunder flashes acting as improvised shells were just part of the introduction. On the ranges you knew when to expect the noise because you were instigating it but here the enemy could and would fire at any time.

Woodland nighttime sorties where booby-traps and small arms fire from specialist sharpshooters could raise the level of tension dramatically even though you knew it was only a practice. In the real thing the enemy's guns would be depressed so that they could aim directly.

If that was not bad enough the lessons that used TEWT at Annan were now put into practice with men and vehicles. The ability to tackle a tank or other enemy vehicle as well as escaping from one under fire were all things that during the ten days of the course had to be taught and practised as the next time it will be for real.

The end of the course arrived on the 9th of November, not too soon, and Jimmie used his pass to get a train back to the relative quiet of training at Porthcawl.

Street Fighting School

Being at Porthcawl was becoming rather like dancing the Hokey Cokey one time he was **'IN'** the camp the next he was **'OUT'** - training elsewhere.

On Thursday 26th November it was time to be **OUT**, out at the Street Fighting School. Somewhat different to the battle school it was a short but highly intensive two-day course of kill or be killed. It was conducted in a street of terraced houses that possibly had been requisitioned in a derelict or bombed area. The rear doors and windows were bricked up so that nothing untoward went in the direction of the neighbours. It was all part of the "fun" to have bullets and brick splinters ricocheting around you. Hand grenades and the Sten-gun were useful weapons for this task although the Sten did have a habit, or knack, of stopping when it shouldn't. Jimmie had to learn to deal with it or risk being killed.

IN again on 28th November to find that it had become difficult to find sufficient volunteers to make a full complement for "C" Squadron. It was hoped that this would be fulfilled by the 1st Belgium Infantry Brigade. However, their Colonel Jean-Baptist Piron decided that they would rather be an independent Belgium force. He had all the required sections available including fully Motorised infantry, armoured cars and artillery as well as various logistical and medical support units. Piron decided in the December of 1942 to leave the 49th Recce and to form what was to become known as the "Brigade Piron".

He took them into Normandy in August '44 and they went on to become one of the first troops into Belgium later that year.

Piron's decision left the squadron under strength. The shortages were eventually found in February the following year utilising the 24th Guards Independent Squadron originally formed in Jimmie's hometown of Wimbledon. When they arrived in Porthcawl and were absorbed into "C" Squadron it brought the Regiment up to full strength.

Christmas was coming and like all the others Jimmie was anticipating time off as he wanted to spend it with his family in Nancy's family home at Belvedere, the first Christmas as a family of three. Much to their delight permission came through for leave starting on Saturday the 19th. The Atlantic frontal system that had crossed the country bringing some periods of very heavy rain had stopped in time for his journey. For the start of his Christmas break some unusually mild weather with temperatures in the low double figures was left behind. Unfortunately, the atmosphere, as well as the weather, got a bit colder as time moved towards Christmas Day as he was ordered to report to the Army Fighting Vehicles School on the 23rd December. His wish to be at home for this his first family threesome Christmas was not to be as his nine day leave had been shortened to only four.

Army Fighting Vehicles School.

There were over twenty Army training schools of various types in the UK by the end of '42 with the main Armoured Fighting Vehicle (AFV) School being at Bovington an ideal and difficult training ground. Situated on the south coast of Dorset on the chalk hills of the Purbeck ridge that extended from Lulworth Cove in the west to where it met the sea at Old Harry Rocks in the east. The school provided driving and maintenance training on the main site with gunnery practice at the firing ranges of Lulworth. The

Bindon range at Lulworth was the only fully equipped AFV range in the country and by the time Jimmie arrived they had at least thirty five different types of AFV on the site with which to train and educate the increasing numbers of troops arriving in the preparation for D-Day. Accommodation space became a major requirement so much so even the local village of Tyneham was sacrificed to the MOD to help in the preparations.

On 23rd December Jimmie was amongst those who reported for duty and so began his real in-depth introduction and use of the various vehicles that were incorporated into the fighting vehicles used by the Recce. To be fleet of foot and still have the ability to pack a punch whilst providing protection meant that a new range of vehicles would be required. The MOD invited tenders for what was to become the armoured car. There were a number of armoured cars produced during the second world war some designs had only a couple of hundred produced, whilst others the production ran into thousands. With speed and agility the main requirement the so-called light armoured cars were popular in the British Army.

The main contender was the Daimler Dingo and it was most probably the most successful in WWII with 6,626 passing through the production lines. The car utilised the most modern technologies, it had a fluid flywheel, preselected gearbox with four-wheel drive and steering that gave it a tight turning circle. The transmission was arranged so that by the operation of a single lever it had 5 forward and 5 reverse gears. The all-wheel steering meant that the drivers had to learn a new technique which some found difficult. Because the difficulty in driving outweighed the advantages of the all-wheel steering the later models reverted to standard front steering only.

Coming as a close second was the Humber Light it had the highest top speed of 75 mph although if the speed governor was removed it was reported that it could achieve 125 mph. The main armament was the Boyes anti-tank rifle which in most cases was superseded by the Bren. A total of 3,400 were built and they were employed in Africa and North West Europe with a number used for airfield defence.

Coming in third position was the Morris Light where 2200 were built having a Boyes rifle as its main armament as the early Humber Lights with their main use being RAF station protection.

Whilst the so-called "lights" fitted the bill for speed and agility it was also deemed necessary to be able to provide a bit of firepower. To be able to stop the opposition and make them think, so the heavies were introduced.

The most popular heavy, was the Humber armoured car by the Rootes Group with 5,400 being built. It was based on the bodywork of the Guy light armoured car fitted to the Karrier K4 van chassis with a rear-mounted power source. A Rootes 6 cylinder petrol engine that developed 90 hp (67 kW) enabled a top speed of 50 mph. It had the ability to be able to easily select either two or four-wheel drive although most of the time it was used in the two-wheel-drive configuration. The turret and fighting compartment were positioned midway between the front and rear axles. It used a 37 mm American gun as the main punch and a long barrel BESA 15mm machine gun which was powerful enough to penetrate up to 10/15mm armour

The Daimler was a good second in popularity, with 2693 being produced and if you were a Daimler man you considered it the best armoured car of the war. It was a parallel development with the Dingo using another Birmingham Small Arms design. Again like the Dingo it was up to date with the latest drive technologies. After the problems with the four-wheel steering on the Dingo, they eventually opted for the more conventional front-wheel steering system. Initially they used the same gearbox as the Dingo but because of its increased weight there was a problem. After a short delay the problem was solved. It still used the Dingo styled gearbox with five forward and reverse gears enabling the car to achieve a top speed of 50 mph, in theory in either direction. Its main punch came from a quickfire 2 lb main gun fitted into a central turret similar to the MkVII Light Tank. For secondary armament they had an 8 mm Besa and 303 Bren machine gun.

If a heavy punch was wanted there was a heavy Heavy in the shape of the AEC which although only 629 were built they did come with a 6 pounder rather than the two pounders of the more popular heavies. It was nicknamed a wheeled tank.

Besides the armoured cars and universal carriers there was also one other armoured vehicle used for the rapid movement and deployment of troops. The American produced M3 Half-Track. Over 54,000 were made and saw service with the allies, including Russia, in all theatres of the Second World War, being especially useful to the Recce. It was a lightweight for an armoured vehicle coming in at only nine tonnes. The saving in weight was mainly achieved by its thin and restricted armour. Vulnerable parts were protected by 12 mm armour plating and the front radiator was protected by armoured grills. Additional protection was provided for the driver by making the windscreen bulletproof. The bulk of the vehicle and those travelling in it were only protected against small arms fire by 6 mm plate but not from heavy-duty machine guns. The top of the back was completely open which left the troop in the back liable to injury from airburst shells. For their defence the M3 was fitted with one or two vehicle-mounted M2 browning or equivalent machineguns. With a top speed of 45 mph it was almost as quick as the armoured cars and with its front-mounted winch it was capable of getting places that the cars couldn't and proved a valuable tool to the assault troops. Variants for mortar troops and HQ personnel were also built.

After seven weeks of hard and intensive work and a lot to learn Jimmie was well up to speed and had been thoroughly introduced to armoured cars a vehicle that was to play such a large part in the next twenty-two months. He could now enter qualification P1 in his Officer's record of Service book and using his return train pass managed to divert via Belvedere for a well deserved eight days leave before returning to Porthcawl.

Humber Light Armoured Car

Humber MkIV Heavy Armoured Car

Chapter 7   Porthcawl

On the 5th September 1942 under Lt Col G.B.King the 49th Reconnaissance Regiment was formed. Their base was in the South Wales town of Porthcawl. The Esplanade Hotel, which was situated right on the front, acted as their main billet housing their Head Quarters, Guard Room and Dining Room. The hotel acquired its name from the wide expanse and esplanade between it and the sea wall. The space was large enough to park a number of their vehicles as well as having sufficient room for the evening Guard Mounting parades taken daily at 1800 hrs. A spectacle watched by a large crowd of onlookers when an Orderly Officer and RSM would inspect the Guard before they moved off to the various vehicle parks about the town.

Most of the troops were trained soldiers who had been in the army either before or since the outbreak of war so to a large extent it was a case of knocking them into shape. Individual fitness was a high priority with intensive physical training being undertaken on the sands with cross country runs over the dunes. As well as physical fitness they also had to learn and practice the new skills required for the Recce. There were gun drill exercises by the anti-tank troop on the Common opposite the Seabank Hotel and a visit to Harlech enabled them to practice on dummy tanks.

It was there that Jimmie was introduced to the Humber MkIV heavy armoured car with the number 41 on a green over gold diagonally split square signifying a reconnaissance vehicle. This was the vehicle that was to become his fighting home. He would have to learn about the vehicle inside and out. The crew of three would practice at each other's job until they became fully proficient and master of all. To bring this newly formed unit up to the required standard training began in earnest. This meant utilisation of the local countryside of the Black Mountains and the Brecon Beacons sixty odd miles away from the town. To get there and back would have meant moving in convoy with the usual share of mistakes along the way as Joe Hoadley a driver of a Carrier from "B" Squadron remembered. He had taken a wrong turn but as the following "C" Squadron passed he managed to join in with them. He was confident that nobody noticed his little escapade since he wasn't rebuked for his error.

Radio communications were of great importance and it was essential that this was fully mastered. The radio and communications were to play a key part in their role and enabled them to provide a phantom net during the battle for Le Havre and later in Holland at the Mark Canal. Another part of their radio work would be used to great effect to call in the infantry or direct gunfire once they had located the enemy. They soon appreciated that a good understanding of radio communications and teamwork was essential.

———————————

A new year dawned with the war going favourably in North Africa. The German armies were in retreat in the Caucasus, the battle for Leningrad was ending and the 49th started preparing in earnest for their invasion of France. The 9th of February saw him with eight days leave to return to Belvedere and his wife and son. Then he applied for and managed to get another nine days leave on the 22nd of April that coincided with his twenty-sixth birthday.

Whilst he was on leave there were changes in the command structure. Their CO Lt Col G.B.King left and at the same time on the 30th April a new GOC took over from Major General Curtis. His replacement was a highly decorated First World War veteran who fought with the Kings Royal Rifle Corps accumulating a DSO, MC and had been mentioned twice in despatches. His name was Evelyn Hugh Barker who soon won the nickname of "Bubbles" Barker as it aptly expressed his effervescent spirit, puckish humour and his high energy that enabled him to move at the double as standard practice stressing his juniors to keep pace.

"C" Squadrons Captain Ken Baker said that he recalled Barker's first visit to the Division where he looked and spoke very much like Monty. He was determined that everyone should be at the peak of physical fitness if they were to play their full part in the invasion. He took exception to the divisional emblem of the Polar Bear with its droopy head down appearance just like the fox advertisement for a popular sweet at the time, (Foxes Glacier Mints). Although, no doubt it was explained to him that when a Polar Bear charges it does so with its head down, he requested that the emblem be changed to something that looked ferocious with a snarl on its face. The emblem was changed much to the chagrin of many tailors that had to replace the old emblem with the new on umpteen uniforms. The new style seemed to convey Barker's message especially to the Germans that soon gained a very healthy respect for the charging head up Polar Bear.

On the 11th May 1943 after a long and hard-won battle in Tunisia Herman Goering surrendered, meanwhile in South Wales Jimmie was promoted to Acting Captain. As tradition dictated he went to the local photographic studios to get a record of this proud time to send home to his mother. He donned his uniform complete with the officer's Sam Browne belt.

> *The Sam Browne belt was named after a then Captain Sam James Browne of the Punjab Cavalry who in a VC winning attack lost his right arm. He designed the belt comprising of the wide traditional belt with a thinner diagonal belt that passed over the right shoulder. This helped to compensate for the difficulty his disability*

caused when wearing his officer's sword. The narrow strap helped to stabilise the scabbard when the sword was worn. The belt was also adopted by his fellow officers but did not become commonly used by the British Army until after he retired.

The diagonal thinner belt passed over his right shoulder and underneath the shoulder straps that were now proudly displaying his three new pips. His lapel badges showed the spear flanked by two lightning flashes confirming the gold and green braid on the shoulder that he was a proud Captain in the Reconnaissance Regiment.

––––––––––––––––

Where there are soldiers and pretty girls the inevitable will happen. In Porthcawl during their stay eleven soldiers were attracted to eleven local girls helping to create that warm relationship between the 49th Recce and the town. In the nearby village of Newton there is a late twelfth-century grade I listed church of St John the Baptist where in the early days of wartime second in command of "C" Squadron Captain Ken Baker met, fell in love and married a local girl.

The timetable of the war meant that their stay in Porthcawl had to come to an end in the spring of '43 as the Polar Bears became part of the 1st corps and were earmarked as an assault division for the invasion. So that summer it was a sad farewell but not a goodbye. The relationship between the town and 49th was to continue in the post-war period when visits to the town were organised. One of these visits was to commemorate, the 50th anniversary of their formation when in the church of St John, the same church in which Captain Baker had married during those dark days a commemorative plaque to that occasion was unveiled.

Unfortunately the old Esplanade Hotel didn't survive long after the war's end it was replaced by the modern looking Esplanade House. On 15th October 2005 Gwyn Petty, Porthcawl Museum Curator, together with Corporal Sid Godfrey of "A" Squadron unveiled a memorial plaque at the entrance to the building. The plaque was designed by Gwyn and made from Welsh slate mounted on Welsh oak. Together with some of the 'old brigade' they gathered in front of the new building on that same piece of pavement where they had paraded 50 years ago. Now in civvies and with medals on their breast they proudly paraded the regimental colours. Their parade as it had in time gone by remained the spectacle it had been years ago and attracted the attention of the locals, some who may have remembered those earlier parades in the far off days of '43 when, in front of the old Esplanade Hotel, the guard was inspected.

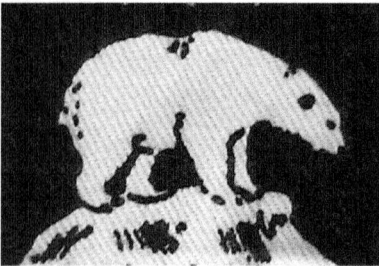

Original Head Down Insignia Changed to Head Up in 1943

Chapter 8 From Assault to Bitter Disappointment

August '43 saw Sicily in allied hands and on Thursday 5th August Jimmie starting another nine days leave. Whilst away his promotion to the war rank of Temporary Captain was confirmed. This was an achievement that made not only Jimmie very proud but also his wife, mother and father, who with his many years of service, would certainly have saluted it.

In October, in preparation for their assault role in the upcoming invasion they moved from the Brecon Beacons in Wales to the Kylsithe Hills in the Kirkintilloch area just north of Glasgow where a more strenuous training was to continue. This was followed by a visit to the area around St Andrews on the east coast of Scotland just south of Dundee for amphibious training. The ability to grease up their vehicles so that they kept running when charging from the landing craft through the sea to the shore became essential. After the occasional soaking and the embarrassment of having to be towed out the knack of greasing up properly was gained. After all, if they stalled in the real thing it could be a short war. Jimmie's war took another nine-day break on the 11th of November for a trip home. Although he didn't know it at the time that was to be the last time Jimmie would see his father. In the following April just a week before his 27th birthday he received the sad news that his father, at the early age of 61, had died from the disability he received whilst serving during the First World War.

After all his training from the early days of May 1934 when he signed up, through all the recent visits to Junior Leaders, Battle School, Street Fighting and finally the long course at the Armoured Fighting Vehicles School let alone the exercises in the Brecon Beacons and most recently the Kylsithe Hills he was to find his military world was about to be shattered. The first blow came just before

Christmas. Monty had returned to the UK after his successes in North Africa to take command of the British forces for the invasion and had decided that he wanted a battle-proven assault force to lead the assault onto Gold Beach in the first wave of the invasion. The shambles of Namos and Åndalsnes was not in the 49[th]s favour so the 50th Tyne Tees was selected to replace the 49th. No doubt there was much relief at Raynes Park and Belvedere that their beloved would not be one of the first into the firing line. As for Jimmie he like most of his fellows was ready for it, they wanted to show Gerry that they were made of sterner stuff than when he last met the 49th in Norway. Their time and opportunity would come soon enough. Until then for the 49th it was back to retraining for their new role as a "Follow up" division. That month they moved to Wolterton Park near Aylsham Norfolk.

Then a cruel and even a more unkind twist of fate happened. He was called in to see his CO who had the bad news for him. There had been a new influx of officers into "C" Squadron and it was Jimmie's misfortune that a Captain of Substantive Rank arrived. Now whether this was anything to do with the elitism of the Guards who formed the core of "C" Squadron or not I don't know. Whether it was the fact that he was from that part of society that didn't have the two things essential to become an officer of Cert A and a bank account neither of which Jimmie originally had, again I don't know. Jimmie was going to be placed on the "Y" list as a reserve to be placed when and where he was required. Jimmie argued his case to remain with the unit in which he had for the last four years trained and gained experience. The end result was that his spell as a Captain was to be short lived as on the 29th December he relinquished his hard earned rank of Captain and returned to his previous substantive rank of Lieutenant. A rank that he held until 19th December 1945 when he was regranted his rank of Captain.

The idea behind the holding group was for it to act as a reservoir and supply centre to replace casualties sustained by the front line. For the army Group 21, the group to which the 49th were attached, there were holding groups numbered 101 thru 105 plus 2 Armoured which had been allotted. From D-day for the following eight days Corps reception camps would be set up at or near the beachheads and the reinforcements sent directly to them from the UK. A small clerical staff from GHQ 2nd Echelon was attached to each Corp Reception Camp and they organised the appropriate distribution of the reinforcements. On D+8 Reinforcement Group 101 landed in Normandy with 6000 men and set up in the area of Bayeaux replacing the earlier beach head groups. Later in July 102 arrived in France. These two groups then followed the advancing troops and were fed from the remaining RHG still based in the UK.

The remaining groups slowly arrived in France, 104 being in Ostend in October handling forward infantry requirements with 105 in Dieppe becoming the source for the recovered injured to be marshalled back to their units via 104.

Although Nancy was very relieved that Jimmie was now in the follow-up division she felt terribly sorry for him as he had to relinquish his hard earned rank of Captain. Jimmie had obviously impressed his superiors with his ability and his arguments so all was not lost. He wasn't to become just a number on a reinforcement list as he was to continue training with them until he was transferred to a Reinforcement Holding Group.

It was to the 105 that Jimmie was allotted and taken on strength on 26th May.

1944 arrived with much anticipation of a pending second front in Europe. The Americans were now involved. They were here, there, in fact everywhere in England, Scotland, Wales and Northern Ireland. Some of the places that Jimmie had passed through since 1940 were now the bases for not only American but also Canadian, Belgium, Dutch and Polish troops. Something big was going to happen it was just a question of when. That something was Operation Overlord, the invasion of Northern Europe. The actual date of the landing was set for sometime in May when the tides and weather were forecast to be favourable. Although the actual timing was kept a secret it was obvious to the Germans that the only place from where there is a short route to occupied Europe was from England. The obvious and shortest route was across the twenty-one miles of the English Channel from Dover to the Pas de Calais which was much the inverse of one of the routes they had selected for their own invasion plans of the postponed Operation Sea Lion in September 1940. They had also selected other crossing points from Cherbourg and Le Havre so they were aware of the military alternatives.

There were some in the German High Command, including Hitler that thought that there was an alternative to the obvious and that area was the coast of Normandy. This was to lead to the strengthening of the coastal defences' further west along the Normandy coast towards the Atlantic.

A great deception plan was instigated by the Allies to convince the Germans that the Pas de Calais was the intended way back into Europe. Jimmie and the 49th Recce became a small part of that deception plan. Although Jimmie and his fellow comrades did not appreciate it at the time, they like a lot of troops being held in reserve became part of the great deception plan code-named Operation Bodyguard. By moving them to holding areas along the south east coast together with inflatable dummy tanks and aircraft they managed to cause sufficient disagreement in the German High Command. This ensured that valuable troops guns and tanks were held ready to defend against an invasion that the German Generals managed to convince Hitler would come across the channel to the Pas de Calais.

As part of the Allies' deception all civilians living within ten miles of the coast were evacuated. There were to be no more home leaves and troops were strictly controlled as to where they could venture. Walls have ears as the advert said so it was essential to reduce the risk of any accidental leaking of information. At Newhaven the local houses along the front had already been demolished by the army in order to deny any invading forces cover.

The British weather then took a hand in the arrangements for Overlord causing a delay to the 5th June which it managed to extend another day. So it was that D-day, was committed to be 6th June 1944 and so become the first day of the beginning of the end to the war in Europe.

Having been replaced as part of the early assault troops "A" Squadron embarked at Yarmouth and started to feel French soil of Gold beach under their boots as early as the evening of 6th June. On 13th June 1 and 7 troops and HQ of "C" Squadron together with "B" Squadron embarked at the Royal Albert Docks with a destination of Item Beach Arromanches.

The rest of "C" squadron went with their vehicles to Norfolk and on 29th June embarked on Empire Celia and Ocean Angel at Tilbury with the Captains' log showing the destination as Normandy. An unpleasant sea crossing awaited them as the worst gales in decades raced up the Channel causing them to have to lay off Southend. Eventually on the 2nd July they were transferred to landing craft and landed near Arromanches when they too joined the rest of the regiment on French soil

For someone that wanted to get involved in the war things weren't going quite the way he expected but a change for the better, as far as he was concerned, was on its way.

Jimmie who had been deprived of his armoured car and now was on the replacement list, attached to Recce Regiment HQ. He made his way with a jeep to Newhaven in Sussex. He arrived by the 1st of June ready to prepare to embark for France but he still had nearly another month to wait. Then it became his turn to grease up his vehicle on the hard concrete standing of Tide Mills before it was loaded on the 24th June as Jimmie and the Recce HQ embarked for Arromanches.

PART TWO

The Real Thing

Chapter 9 First Blooding

On the 6th June 1944 the secret was out. 4000 ships and many tens of thousands of fighting troops from America, Canada, Europe, the United Kingdom and its Empire were taking, for the first time in France, the war on the ground directly to the Germans.

Since the 50th Tyne Tees had taken over the assault role, the Polar Bears could only wait in anticipation for their turn. The 49th Division was an early arrival in France after the initial assault troops. It was "A" squadron of the Recce who were the first ashore late on the 6th June followed four days later by the Regimental Head Quarters, "B" Squadron and only a part of "C" Squadron, their Head Quarters together with 1 & 7 Troop. The sea was running wild on the lead up to a major storm on the 19th and was causing problems with the landing. 1 Troop managed to get ashore on Item Beach on 16th June with 7 Troop having to wait it out at sea until the following day. 1 & 7 troops then went on to make their first harbour at Brouay before going into action with "A" Squadron. They had carried out a sweep across a cornfield towards the Fontenay Road to find it occupied by a German 88mm gun who objected to their presence for a short time. On the 30th June "C" Squadron suffered their first casualty when during a little skirmish Sergeant Preston was wounded and had to be evacuated.

Meanwhile, the rest of "C" Squadron had to wait for the worst June gale for nearly half a century in the English Channel to abate. During these storms dozens of vessels were sunk at sea and about 800 were wrecked on the Normandy shores. One mulberry harbour had been wrecked and damage had been sustained by the other making landing difficult.

Sections of the Mulberry harbour build from concrete and steel were floated over late on D-Day and were installed in the bay at Arromanches to form a harbour about the same size as Dover Harbour is today. Sixty years later the remains of the mulberry harbour still adorn the beaches and bay, a tribute to all that designed, manufactured, brought and installed it all that time ago in the hazardous conditions of war.

Beyond the outer elements of the mulberry that can still be seen today there would have been the outer breakwaters or Gooseberries composed of sunken merchantmen, none of which have survived, their job completed they were broken up for scrap.

Because the earlier storm damage the mulberry harbour at Arromanches had not been fully repaired by the time Jimmie arrived he was transferred to a landing craft offshore beaching just east of the harbour on 2nd July. Moving off the beach to spend his first night at Le Hamel, a small coastal village that the month before was the site of some stout resistance to the invading forces.

The following day the balance of "C" Squadron had established itself. They left Le Hamel and following the taped safe routes to avoid mines moved inland towards the front line and action. On the 3rd of July the complete "C" Squadron harboured at Brouay with the rest of the Regiment and were ready for the next move towards St Pierre.

Three kilometres to the west of them was the town of Audrieu and half a kilometre south on the Rue de Tilly was a Chateau by the same name which until a few weeks before was the headquarters of General Kurt Meyer commander of the 12th SS Panzer Division. It was while Jimmie and the rest of the 49th Recce were waiting to embark for Normandy that one of the defining moments for the Polar Bears occurred here. In the local skirmishes with the 49th West Riding Infantry and the Canadian Winnipeg Rifles some 40 had been taken prisoner by the Germans and taken to the chateau. The war grew closer to the chateau and eventually it stood in no man's land. It was hit by twenty-seven 105 mm shells and several anti-tank shells shot it through and through but the Caen stone proved to be tough. The building resisted valiantly, today it shows only a few traces of that heroic and bloody period. Unfortunately the trees in the area did not escape from the brutal treatment of the shelling, many had to be cut down and those that remain today are riddled with shell splinters and shrapnel that penetrated the wood to a depth of 40 centimetres. There are big bulges and deep gashes rimmed with lip-shaped excrescences on the trunks outlining the traces of those deep wounds. Every year, even now, some of them die from the long struggle against the cancer that ate away at their inside.

When the battle was won a section of the 757 Field Company, Royal Engineers were clearing the street and verges of mines when an old lady informed them that there were a number of British soldiers buried in the grounds of the chateau. In the shadow of the wall that surrounded the chateau shallow graves were found. On exhuming the bodies they found 14 Canadians from the Regina Rifles and the rest were from the 49th. All had their hands tied behind their backs and had been shot through the head. Although the local civilians said the atrocity had been committed by Russian soldiers attached to the German Army the men of both divisions swore that they would not take another SS prisoner alive. A week or so later after the battle for Rauray the traitor Lord Haw Haw broadcasting from Germany called the 49th "The Polar Bear Butchers". A British postcard at the time showed a Polar Bear with one forepaw sweeping aside German tanks whilst with another stabbing soldiers on a butcher's block, captured the troop's feelings. This was not going to be another Norway!

Meyer was captured in September '44 and later tried at the Canadian War Crimes Commission. Found guilty he was sentenced to death but this was commuted to life imprisonment on the grounds that it could not be definitely proved that he actually gave the order for the executions.

He was released in September 1954 and died of a heart attack on 23rd December 1961.

"THE BUTCHER"

Initially the Recce could not be used in the role that it had been trained but took on an inactive role of defence in depth providing flank protection between St Pierre and Rauray, which had the two main unpleasant disadvantages of living dug-in and receiving the attention of regular German shell fire. Besides enemy action unfortunately there was also what is euphemistically called battle accidents. On 10th July Trouper Longley was the first to be injured in one such incident.

The Bocage countryside with its narrow lanes and high hedges atop steep banks was not suitable country for the armoured cars of the Recce. The role for which he and his fellows had trained so long and so hard was still to avoid them, but the war didn't. The Bocage had to be cleared the hard way by boots on the ground. Little victories ebbed and flowed as the Germans made it difficult and often counterattacked. Extreme caution was needed since the Bosche were quite adept at hiding in the thick hedgerows until patrols had passed and then shooting at them from behind. A lot of tough fighting resulted in casualties and today beside the road from Fontenay to Rauray proudly stands a memorial to the men of the 49th Division, the Polar Bears who fought here in that June of 1944. On that memorial is a plaque remembering the 49th Reconnaissance Corps.

For the next few weeks the Recce had the infantry role of guarding and protecting vital crossroads in this region. Then on July 19th they took over from the infantry in Tessel Wood. Today the wood is not as large as it was then and fresh trees have replaced those denuded of their foliage by the shellfire of 1944. The enemy was close at hand. It was here in this region that Jimmie got his first taste of battle. Gone were the days of training, this was the real thing and unlike their training offices firing live rounds over their heads the German's aim was lower and they were playing for keeps. Jimmie recalls that in his first real firefight all he could remember that he just wanted to get as close to and bury himself into the ground as much as possible. Yes, the training at Battle School last October had prepared him for the noise and confusion of battle. But knowing that their opposite number was waiting on the other side of a bush or tree and aiming lower than the sergeants at Birmingham with the direct intention to kill brought a frightening reality to the situation. Later, once he had learned the difference in the sound between friendly and hostile fire and also appreciate that not every shot was aimed at him the fear became manageable but it never left him.

The eeriness of the wood where the undergrowth was unusually thick made it impossible for silent movement of the night patrols. The trees creaked in the wind in a ghostly fashion heightening the tension ensuring that patrols sometimes returned to the Command Post wreathed in perspiration.

Without too much trouble today's visitors can find the remains of many unused German stick grenades, mortars and other general paraphernalia of war in and around the wood. Some are in piles around the edge of the fields collected by the farmers when they tilled them out of the soil as they claimed some of the woodlands of '44. For those of a more intrepid nature, a metal detector in the remaining woods can often find unspent munitions.

On 21st July they left Tessel Wood and were transferred from the 30 Corps area to that of 1 Corps, north and north east of Caen. On the 24th they moved at night to the left flank of the Bridgehead across some rough country to Capelle.

They then moved in convoy around the north of Caen crossing the River Orne using Pegasus Bridge and were placed under the command of 146th Infantry Brigade and went on to harbour at the town of Touffreville. On the 2nd August they were subjected to heavy shelling during which for "C" Squadron; Sergeant Walter Pettit, Sergeant Robert McGill, Corporal Harry Eastwood, together with Private Albert Duquemin of the army catering corps became their first fatalities with three others wounded and three more during the following days shelling.

The stormy weather of June followed by the heat of July proved to be a good breeding ground for another enemy, a much smaller enemy that was airborne. The Luftwaffe was dangerous when flying whilst this particular smaller enemy became an annoyance when not, the Mosquito. Their role as infantry continued as they moved into the Ranville area where the 6th Airborne Division were engaged in their part of the war against the seventy-three tanks of 22nd Panzers. The Germans had taken up position in Chicheboville Wood out of sight of prying RAF reconnaissance flights. The Recce took up positions to protect the 6th's flanks as they moved forward.

It was no fun fighting as infantry and they were desperate to start the war that they had trained for. On the 10th of August, their wish came true, the first Recce patrol was carried out. It passed through "B" Squadron towards

Vimont where as it approached open fields just south west of the town it ran into trouble when one of the carriers was hit by an enemy 88 mm gun. Later that same day enemy shelling of the squadron harbour at Chicheboville killed George Wood. Two days later the casualty list increased again as in another shelling John Greenwood was killed. On the 13th of August they had their first face to face meeting with the enemy, a deserter from the 981st Grenadiers of the 272nd Infantry division decided that the war had gone on long enough and was too dangerous for him. With his empty hands aloft he surrendered.

The little forays forward continued over the next few days and then reports by patrols on the night of 14th/15th August indicated that the Germans had withdrawn from the 49th Division's front. "C" Squadron was then able, at last, to put their training into practice. Conditions were ideal and the Recces were in their element. Fast mobile warfare, probing forward to establish contact, holding that contact until the infantry arrived. The countryside in this part of France was more like slowly rolling rises than hills. Although not high enough to provide defensive positions they were sufficient to lose an 88 mm gun in a cornfield as a rearguard to inflict losses in men and machines and cause a hiccup in the advance. Over the coming week most of the advance involved dashes from one newly formed bridgehead at one river crossing to the next river where another bridgehead would be established. Once the bridgehead was established the Recce would pass through and probe forward again to the next resistance. The 49th Recce advanced rapidly negotiating blown bridges and mines. Their training was being put into practice and worked. The only real resistance they met was at Mezidon on the river Dives where good training or not the war ended for Gordon Pickford who was killed whilst directing his car through a minefield. Mines proved to be the biggest cause of attrition in this short period. "C" Squadron alone lost twelve wounded and six killed. After some six weeks in Normandy and by the first time they had been used truly as reconnaissance troops they had lost by direct enemy action six of their number to shell fire and one in action.

The scene now was set for the regiment's dash to the Seine over the next two weeks. The advance to the seine was more like their training at home but this time it was a case of "Only the enemy in front with every other bugger behind". There was, however, a bugger in their behind they could have done without. The mosquitoes had now been replaced by another debilitating enemy, dysentery. The problem was not limited to just one squadron for about a month the whole division suffered from a bad bout. The war did not stop for this inconvenience but was slowed by perhaps the biggest problem that faced the Recce, Mines. These not only affected foot patrols but also vehicles and being in a vehicle was no guarantee of personal safety as Trooper Leslie found out when his carrier ran over a mine.

In extraordinary times it is often said that ordinary people do extraordinary things and so it was during the rainy period that had set in towards the end of August. The Germans were falling back and as they did so they left behind small groups in strategic positions to act as a rearguard. Nestling in the open countryside 5 Km north of Lisieux and 1.8 Km east of the 12 m wide River Torque and atop a rise of 110 metres is the village of Norolles. Its position giving it the best observation point in the area and there waited a German anti-tank platoon. The D98 as it is today is the main route from the river through Norolles and as it climbs it follows the gentle sweeping contours of the hillside. The side of the road is typically French with hedgerows bordering the road and the occasional group of trees. The hedges were only low and did not obscure the view from the turret of a Humber Heavy armoured car, for the Humber light, on the other hand, the view was a bit more restricted. Its advantage was that it did provide good ground cover for the antitank platoon. The Germans knew that the Torque had been crossed and were expecting a probe eastwards to locate their positions. They had observed the movement in the valley below and had spotted the turrets of an armoured car patrol that had selected to turn onto the D98 in their direction. They set up an ambush locating themselves in the hedgerow just after a bend so that they had a good strike position. The effective range of the panzerfäust was only 60 metres so they chose their spot to give themselves a good chance of a hit whilst trying to ensure that the second vehicle would not be able to give them additional grief whilst they made their escape from the resultant flying debris arising from a hit.

With the successful crossing of the river Torques two miles north of Lisieux number 3 Troop, which Jimmie was later to command, was patrolling forward. It was getting dark and it was still raining. They were doing their job, seeking out the enemy or to put it another way, looking for trouble. The high ground had always been an army's vantage point and in this area that was the village of Norolles. Operating under code Orange as they expected to find opposition the patrol climbed the slight incline approaching the little village. They were travelling with caution and the four armoured cars were spaced accordingly. In the troop there were two Humber Heavies and two Humber Lights. On this particular occasion a Light was acting as lead car under the command of Corporal Corrall. Trouper Neal sat on the right above his two fellows his Bren gun loaded ready for immediate action. His head protected by the sides of the open-fronted turret. The driver Trooper Doran was sitting in the driver's seat below and in front on the right of the others his head pressed forward against the bump strip to enable him to get the best vision of the road ahead, the pouring rain and the darkening weather were presenting difficult conditions for driving as well as observation. This evening he was reliant on Neal sitting a metre higher than he was with a view unimpeded by the armoured glass in the forward driving slit, his only problem being the rain driven into his eyes by the combination of the wind and the forward movement of the car.

Beside the road camouflaged by the grass and bushes the anti-tank team waited. They could hear the roar of the 4.1 litre six inline cylinder side valve engine producing most of its 60 KWatts of power as it drove its three tonnes of the armoured plated vehicle up the incline. They could not hear the clank of a tracked vehicle so they knew it was an armoured car approaching. They settled down, panzerfäust ready, they had designated as the kill zone a point 50 metres in front of their position and waited.

As Doran drove round a slow right-hand bend the road ahead appeared to be clear of any opposing tank or 88mm gun, and through the intercom Neal confirmed. He started to accelerate keeping a wary eye cast downwards seeking signs of mines.

When the car was 60 metres away the panzerfäust operator stepped from his cover position onto the side of the road tucked the tube under their arm and aimed by aligning the target, the sight, and the top of the warhead. With the aim steady and on target the pedal-like lever, as opposed to a trigger, near the projectile was squeezed, the propellant ignited and 6.8 Kg of hell, death and destruction was on its way.

In less than a second from when Doran's mind registered the puff of smoke from the two-metre backblast as the missile was fired that his world dramatically lurched with a noise like having left your head inside Big Ben when it struck. This was something battle school had not enlightened him on; what it was like to be inside a vehicle when it was hit by a panzerfäust. It was only a matter of seconds later, his ears still ringing from the explosion, when he started to cope with the realisation that the car had been hit. He glanced over his shoulder to see the gunner Neal was slumped immobile in his position and was correctly assessed as having his next leave cancelled. The Smell of cordite and hot metal filled the inside of the car. In a rearward glance he also saw that Corrall was wounded and couldn't get out. The panzerfäust was a once and once only weapon so the danger lay if there was another weapon available or whether the firer of that weapon had beat a discrete escape. He hoped for the latter as he took the decision that the only way to save Corrall was to drive the car back to safety. With his ears still suffering from the noise of the explosion he could not hear if the engine was running. There was no place to turn, forwards was not an option, to reverse meant using the wing mirrors which were already covered in raindrops. The choice was limited so he engaged reverse, discovered the engine was still running and slowly and calmly using the hand throttle backed the Humber down the road and round the bend to where the rest of the patrol was waiting.

Corrall and Doran were taken to the nearest field dressing station and on to hospital where, unfortunately, the following day Doran succumbed to his very bad leg wounds. For his determination and gallant effort he was recommended for and was posthumously awarded on the 15th November 1944 the Military Medal. 14397222 Trooper A.T. Doran MM a proud moment for his family in their loss that is remembered by the words they placed on his gravestone

"GREATER LOVE HAS NO MAN THAN THIS. THAT A MAN LAY DOWN HIS LIFE FOR HIS FRIENDS"

It was incidents like this where the casualties were replaced by those willing and able from the Reinforcement Holding Groups. Although Jimmie wished his fellow officers no ill he was anxious to get into a forward and active position. To put into practice all those years of preparation and training, to get into action, action that he had wanted to see since he joined up ten years ago in the spring of 1934.

Chapter 10   A Well Deserved R&R

The Germans were falling back fast and the 49th Recce was chasing them hard and faster. Well, it was faster between bridges. Most bridges were blown up as the Germans retreated if they weren't then there was a good chance they were booby-trapped. Caution had to be exercised and the Recce often had the bridges and the surrounding area sussed out by the time the sappers arrived. Most of the rivers in this part of France were more large brooks but a water obstacle irrespective of size slowed the advance down. Although distances covered were not great it was a long hard slog in the advance towards the Seine. Not only was it 'build a bridge a day' there was also the detection and lifting of mines and the task of filling in the craters created by the artillery of both sides. By the 24th August they had advanced 20 Km to the river at a place called Calonne to the east of Épaignes.

Épaignes was an ordinary French town whose population had been dwindling over the past two centuries and in 1944 its population had declined from over two thousand to 850 people. Why it had been chosen by the Germans as the town for a strong rearguard action has been lost in the annuls of time but with their backs getting closer to the Seine the Germans were running out of manoeuvring room and decided that Épaignes was a place to make a determined stand. The problem that the Germans faced by taking that decision was that the 49th Recce was on its way to the Seine via Pont Audemer and that Épaignes was on the way. The night patrols had reported back about the defensive positions that had been formed so the GOC decided that the defences were strong enough to warrant a three squadron attack the next day. It was now up to Major Harry Judge to take his first major decision after taking over command of "C" Squadron earlier that evening.

The following morning 4 to 7 troops were in position for the off with the Armoured car troops 1 to 3 held in reserve to provide additional firepower as and when. Planning, tactics, training and what little experience they had came together with the result that the battle at Épaignes was not only their first major battle but also their best. "C" Squadron alone inflicted over 100 casualties and took more than 30 prisoners. Alas, it was not without the loss of trooper Donald Christmas with Sergeant C Watling, Corporal J Bott and Troopers J Black, T Grunshaw, S Hart and W Radcliffe all being wounded.

Following the battle there was a rapid and uneventful advance to the Seine. "A" Squadron had reached Quillebeuf on the Seine and "B" Squadron stopped at Vieuxport also on the Seine but 5 Km further upstream. Their tally of prisoners ran into three figures for very few casualties in the 49th. "C" Squadron linked up with the 6th Airborne Division at Pont Audemer and then went on to harbour in the liberated village of Les Préaux. As the villages were liberated the French civilians appeared with white flags, kept no doubt from 1940, and bottles of Brandy and wine they had hidden from the Germans. It seemed that the whole population wanted to climb aboard, for some reason the armoured cars seemed to act as a magnet to the girls who clung to them crying. In the streets RAF types in blue overalls, clogs and French berets appeared saying they had been fighting with the Maquis. This was a new experience to the Recce boys as it was usual following a town or village's liberation that the Recce moved on to evict the Germans from the next town or village and the following troops reaped the benefit of the liberation celebrations. At Les Préaux whilst still patrolling up to the Seine assessing the enemy's positions and strength they returned to base and were able to take full advantage of and enjoy the great hospitality shown by the locals.

The fight elsewhere in North East Europe was going well. The battle for Paris that had been raging since the 19th of August came to its climax on the 25th when Charles de Gaulle accepted the German surrender.

The next task for the 49th Recce was to clear the Forest of Brotonne, which nestled in one of the largest bends of the Seine, halfway between Rouen and Le Havre, as it flowed on the final stages to the channel. Consequently any remaining Germans were trapped in 120 sq Km of dense forest with limited crossing points of the river available to them. It fell to "C" Squadron to lead the way in the clearing operation.

It was not going to be an easy task, the forest was very thick and whilst there were tracks that ran through the trees it wasn't crisscrossed by roads as it is today. It was a slightly undulating ground rising fairly steeply from the Seine in the west to 140 metres and sloping down to 40 metres as it finally drops back down to the river in the east and north with undulations in between. Maps were of no help, patrol reports told of very dense undergrowth and trees with the earlier forages into the forest confirming that it was too easy to get disorientated and run the risk of becoming casualties from friendly fire. The armoured cars and carriers were not capable of forging their own path indeed on some of the tracks there was only a limited arc of turn possible with the Heavy's main gun. The solution as far as Major Judge was concerned was to take to the air, he would not be able to spot a camouflaged enemy but he would be able to guide and direct his own forces. As fortune would have it an Auster light aircraft was available and Judge was soon airborne. With 1 Troop leading, the column started to make progress advancing under Code Red; the enemy was present. It wasn't to be long before they made that presence known by letting loose a panzerfäust at the lead armoured car ending Corporal Charles Woollaston's war and sending Sergeant J Jardine and Trooper A McKay to the hospital. By evening they had cleared the area to the Seine taking sixty prisoners in the process. Despite Judge's earlier attempt to limit friendly fire casualties, that evening possibly in disbelief that the Recce could have made it to the river the Command group came under a heavy concentration of friendly artillery fire. Fortunately it only resulted in Troopers W Nash and J Morphett being wounded. The following day a reverse sweep was carried out this time with Major Judge's feet on the ground. There were no incidents and only a few German stragglers were found to encourage acceptance of POW hospitality.

On a broad front the Seine had been reached and a bridgehead at Vernon had been achieved. Armour flooded through the 11th (Black Bull) Armoured Division charged north towards Antwerp, the Guards towards Brussels and the Dessert Rats to Ghent. The 49th as part of Monty's left flank had a different job to do. Arromanches was now 180 Km to the rear, whilst PLUTO was being wound out behind the advancing forces all the ammunition, food, medical supplies and troops (fresh and wounded) had to make that long journey. New landing ports had to be opened up in order to shorten the supply route. Le Havre on the right side of the Seine was designated as an important objective and it was the unsung heroes of the Recce that lead the way.

The port of Le Havre was a formidable place to attack as it was one of the strongest fortresses of the Atlantic Wall. It was heavily defended against the major perceived direction of attack from the sea. Large well positioned and protected coastal batteries had been installed to take on that attack but they were only capable of firing seaward. It had natural protection from attack from the land since three sides were surrounded by water. There was the sea to the west, the Seine estuary to the south and a low lying area to the east which had been flooded. The high ground to the north was backed up by anti-tank ditches. Although the land defences were incomplete they were still substantial as there was only one obvious way by land into the port. In the town there were two forts, many roadblocks, pillboxes and fortified houses, supported by 76 field, medium and anti-aircraft guns. The strength of the garrison was estimated at between 8000 and 11000 troops of all types including 1300 naval personnel all under the command of Col Eberhard Wildermuth.

Having reached Quillebeuf "A" Squadron discovered that the only way across the river was by raft. They managed to find two damaged German rafts and started on their repair. Meanwhile a local had offered Bob Faxton of the anti-tank troop to row six of them across the half a kilometre wide river in his small wooden boat. Bob together with his section took up the offer. Having looked at the boat and the river Bob decided that if it came to having to swim at some stage it would be better to unclip his webbing. Once safely with their feet on the dry land of the opposite bank they marched north for four kilometres to a town called Lillebonne where they were met by a strong force of Resistance fighters. Patrols were organised and a defensive position at the crossroads was manned until the rest of the squadron were safely over.

Whilst Bob was busy on the right side of the river the remaining 80 men and twelve vehicles were ferried across, unfortunately one of the rafts capsized and sank with the loss of two carriers and two Free French fighters, the rest arrived safely and linked up with Bob.

Having completed their return sweep of the forest and after a little clear up exercise at Les Goharaux "C" Squadron moved off in the direction of Rouen arriving at its half-collapsed bridge at midnight on 1st/2nd September. The sky was overcast and not conducive to easy driving since the clouds had blotted out all the natural light and navigation especially over the wreck of the bridge was difficult. The boys from the anti-aircraft brigade came to the rescue and shone their searchlights onto the clouds such that the dispersed light generated a form of artificial moonlight quite adequate to drive by.

The Recce was the first to arrive on the northern outskirts of Le Havre once again sampling the civic delights offered by the towns of Goderville and Criquetot. For 1 & 4 Troops it was a sad time as they had to leave the champagne and the specially brewed Benedictine and go out on patrols to the edge of Le Havre's defences. It was not all sad as they returned after having let their presence be felt with twenty-four prisoners. With the arrival of the heavies and the marching army the Recce's job was done and on the 5th September they went into Divisional reserve for rest and reorganisation in the town of La Remuée where they were treated as was usual in France at that time. It was in rests like this that Jimmie was able to use his basic French "Avez vous des oeufs pour le soldat", no doubt there were other phrases used but that is all to which he has admitted.

"Bubbles" Barker had won his spurs in the First World War rising to a Brigade Major by 1918 collecting the Military Cross, Italian Silver Medal for Valour, DSO and had been mentioned in despatches twice which equalled the number of times he had been wounded. He was acutely aware of the mental strain that bombing and shellfire could achieve on the enemy and put this into practice in Le Havre. There were many RAF raids and by this time in the war the accuracy of their bombing had improved. In between raids the navy would add to the stress. He studied the German response time after raids and would deliberately bring in a second raid to disincentivise them in coming out of their deep and safe shelters. After several days of preparatory skirmishes and bombing, a white flag appeared and hopes were raised that surrender was imminent and a bloodless victory would be achieved. Two German envoys accompanied the flag and brought with them a letter from their Commandant the contents of which explained that Hitler has personally ordered the defence of Le Havre to the last man and the last round. The reply from General Barker of "I wish you good luck and a Merry Christmas" left the German Envoys totally mystified not understanding the implication that Bubbles was prepared to keep bombing them until Christmas.

General Barker was one for utilising the best attributes of his forces. In Northern Europe he used the Recce in one of their prime roles of search, find and hold at Le Havre he intended to use their other attribute, their ability for good sound communications. With their R&R shortened they were brought back out of reserve to set up a phantom wireless net of 15 stations covering every unit to help the GOCs' information network.

There was practice at street fighting and Jimmie's experience at the Street Fighting School helped him to train others in the art. Weaponry was changed to include more grenades and sten guns to ensure that they had the best advantage in the struggle to come of taking Le Havre street by street.

By the 10th September Barker judged that the Germans return from their shelters was sufficiently delayed and the ground battle commenced. It was a hard-fought battle with some of the opposition taking Hitler's instruction literally. By the 12th of September those that had followed Hitler's command were dead, those 7,000 that hadn't were prisoners of war. Unfortunately during this time some 5,000 French civilians also died. After the battle the necessary repairs to the bomb damaged port took until the 1st of November before it could start helping the allied war effort and by that time the fighting had moved on and other ports came into play.

Chapter 11   Belgium & Into Holland

After the last shot was fired in anger at Le Havre the fighting forces made way for the sappers and engineers to bring some safety and order back to the harbour area in particular and help out in the town in general. For the fighting troops after having cleaned their weapons, buffed their boots and polished their badges together with a well deserved sleep they found that the war had left them behind. On the 17th of September they saw the great aerial armada flying on their way north east. Many of the planes were towing gliders, two or even three at a time. The armada filled the skies for nearly ten minutes and the roar of aircraft could be heard as an angry drone above that of their own engines. Although they did not know then the planes and their human cargo were destined for the ill-fated attack on Arnhem as part of Operation Market Garden.

To catch the fighting up they had to take the long journey across the north of France through Upper Normandy harbouring at the little French town of Guerville before passing into Picardy, where the roses were shining and then the Pas de Calais. This was the ground that Jimmie's father and his comrades had fought and died over a quarter of a century earlier. This time the Germans weren't standing firm they were on the run, they were being defeated again. The Regiment was travelling in column so the going was slow compared with the Recce's normal speed. It took to the 21st to reach just south of Brussels where they harboured for the night. From there they went on another 55 Km to Harenthout arriving the following day. Five kilometres in front of them was their next objective the Albert Canal named after King Albert I of Belgium. This formidable obstacle was only completed in 1939; the 129 Km multilane water highway from the industrial heartland of Liege to the port of Antwerp was designed to reduce the time taken to get goods to the port. It was not until after the war that it eventually came to realise that objective, reducing the shipping time from 7 days on the older Meuse-Scheldt canal to just 18 hours. In 1944 the Albert Canal, like all the others were obstacles in the drive across Belgium and Holland both for the Axis and Allied forces. The subtle difference was that the bridges behind the Germans were intact which enabled easier movement of men and machines whilst for the Allies the bridges had been destroyed which slowed their advance. This gave the Germans time to make new defensive lines before the next canal. Thus the speed of advance over the canals depended on the infantry to secure a bridgehead and the sappers to provide a bridge until then the advance stopped. There were always those that did it differently; the 49th Recce.

Having moved up to have a look at the canal they realised the enormity of its 100 metres in width with a depth of 3.4 metres compared to the brooks they had crossed in France. This did not deter the assault troop leader Lieutenant J B Tallack of 7 Troop together with Lieutenant A B Hargreaves-Brown troop leader of 4 Troop. They decided to boat across the canal to complete an evaluation of the opposition. Having found that it had melted away they then moved forty men from the two troops across the canal by boat. Once on the other side they deprived the locals of their means of transport as they requisitioned forty of their bicycles. They then pursued the enemy for 15 Km to the outskirts of Oostmalle. The rest of "C" Squadron opted to cross via a Canadian bridge near Antwerp and went on to catch up with the bicyclised 7 Troop at Vosselaar, west of Turnhout.

When "B" Squadron arrived at the Albert Canal near Herentals they soon discovered that all the bridges were destroyed. There was no obvious way across. Lieutenant George Bowman found a solution. In his searching of the area he came across two young ladies who were very pleased to see him and communicated to him that the Germans had left. They told him about a metal scrap yard and on investigation he found that there were a number of substantial girders which George thought could be used as a temporary measure to bridge the gap between the two sections that were left standing of one of the existing bridges. He found some more help from a couple of local men who arrived at the scrap yard with some horses. With a lot of hard work, not only by the horses, the girders were dragged to the canal and a secure but temporary bridge was made. "B" Squadron arrived on the north bank and went on to officially liberate Herentals receiving the adulation of the locals. On the 24th they had moved on and liberated Turnhout.

The 49th Recce were still in Belgium approaching the Dutch Border, Eindhoven was 40 Km to the west as they continued to push north. For "C" Squadron one circle was almost completed when they were joined by a band of Belgium Patriots. No, they weren't the "Brigade Piron" that had left them short in Porthcawl. This was another group of 40 that fought well for them and were incorporated into "C" Squadron and became known as "B" Troop or the Belgium Brigade.

The progress towards their next objective of Rijckevorsal was two kilometres beyond the Dessel–Turnhout–Schoten canal a 63 Km long strip of water that looped northwards from The Albert Canal near Maastricht rejoining it outside Antwerp. The Germans had been thorough this time and ensured that all the bridges and barges were unusable so the advance stopped until the sappers could place bridges over the canal. The time lost enabled the Germans to build a much more robust defensive line before the Mark canal, the next dividing strip of water, with the power within it to strike back.

The building of bridges became much slicker and therefore quicker thanks to Donald C. Bailey a civilian Civil Engineer who worked for the British Army at the Experimental Bridge Establishment (EBE) of the Royal Engineers. His brainchild called in his honour was the Bailey Bridge. The

Bailey bridge came in a variety of formats and was essentially a Meccano set of angles and girders capable of being transported by lorry and bolted together on site to build a bridge able to let an army cross short or narrow water obstructions. With bridges built "C" Squadron moved across and liberated Rijckevorsal where they made their base during a lull in the advance.

———————————————

Five kilometres to the west "B" Squadron also crossed the same canal and advanced on the town of Sint Lenaarts. In the Lead or "Aunt Sally" position was Joe Hoadley who we have met last in Porthcawl when he lost his squadron and joined in with "C" on the way back from the Brecons. He had swapped his carrier for a Humber Light and was now approaching Sint Lenaarts from the canal along Pothoek towards Kerkstraat. There was plenty of debris and equipment including hundreds of stick grenades scattered all over the road from a previous German encounter with a Typhoon. As he arrived at the junction with Kerkstraat he found himself on higher ground with a fine view of the church with open ground below and to the right. He proceeded on towards the church and the town centre leaving behind him the shelter of the local houses. He was now in open ground with drainage ditches on either side between him and the fields. The next thing Joe knew was the ear deafening and stunning roar of an explosion. Slowly through the struggling senses he could hear someone shouting "Bail out!" It was an easy command but as the driver for Joe to be able to bail out he had to slide his seat back, open the door and then roll out. As he hit the ground the place came alive with machine guns, bullets whizzing everywhere as though the whole world and his dog was trying to kill him. Joe kept as low as he could using the car for as much protection as possible until he realised that it might brew and explode. Unfortunately for Joe on the side of his car where he had bailed out there was no ditch to hide in. He started to crawl back the way he had come when there was a lull in the shooting.

Joe surveyed the road and noticed a short and shallow water filled ditch just ahead. He looked to his left and contemplated trying to make a dash across the road but decided the ditch was the safer bet and so he got wet.

The firing had stopped he used the time to gather his thoughts. His commander Corporal Stoddard and gunner Trooper Taylor were nowhere to be seen. He called out but there was no reply; "bought it" he thought. The rest of the squadron were giving the Germans stick in the hope that any survivors from the stricken car could make it back. Eventually they came under heavy and accurate fire and had to fall back 400 metres to a position of cover. After a couple of hours the heavy brigade arrived and then another attempt was made to move up the road and incurred the loss of two of their number. Eventually Sint Lennarts was taken and Stoddard and Taylor were recovered slightly wounded but otherwise okay. A search was carried out for Joe but he was not found so he was listed as missing.

As Joe told later he had bailed out on the right-hand side of the car and his two fellow crew members chose the left hand side. They made it back whilst he, after playing doggo in the ditch, ended up having a friendly chat with three German soldiers with his hands in the air. He subsequently spent the rest of the war doing his best to annoy the Germans from a POW camp. Joe claimed the accolade of being the first man that his CO Lieutenant G Bowman had lost in that way.

Operation Market Garden had ended in a disaster having failed to meet its objectives but like Dunkirk as the allies managed to save a high proportion of the troops it was soon classified as a triumph. For the 49th Recce there was no forward movement but that did not mean that there was no movement. Together with the Canadians they made several sweeps through enemy held territory inflicting considerable casualties and taking 300 prisoners. Alas casualties were not one sided. The fearless Lieutenant A B Hargreaves-Brown and his mortar sergeant, Sergeant Wilfred (Pincher) Martin were killed by shellfire whilst conducting an artillery shoot. During this action Trooper Milligan went missing to be later confirmed as a POW and Trooper Picton won his Military Medal. Hargreaves-Brown, known as Sandy, was an archetypal Scottish Laid who when in England would walk around with a shepherd's crook. Before leaving for France he wrote his will in such a way that everyone in his troop became a beneficiary. The amounts varied from £50 to £550 dependant on rank and time served in the troop. One of the members of his troop was Tom Debnam. He had been with Hargreaves-Brown since 1941 when the 24th Independent Reconnaissance Regiment was formed and received £550 plus an additional amount of £2500. Sandy was the type of leader that men respected and this was evident by the tributes that adorned his battlefield grave marked by a simple wooden cross on the edge of the field where his best endeavours ceased.

September moved into October and the 49th moved into Holland. The speed of their advance slowing as the Germans struck up some defensive positions before each major canal until that position crumbled. The sequence of retreating to prepare another line of defence before the next canal continued. The closer the defensive line got to their Fatherland the stronger and more determined became their defensive lines. The fighting was now getting more intense with casualties mounting daily. By now Jimmie's attributes were coming to the fore and he was earmarked for promotion to a Troop Leader. In the latest round of reorganisation the promotion was to miss him, it was now just a matter of a little more time; like waiting for dead or wounded man's shoes; not a very pleasant thought but such is war.

On 6th October "C" Squadron was in outpost positions just over the Dutch border near German occupied Poppel Wood. At 14.00 hrs just as they were to hand over to the Lincolns they were attacked by the 6th German Parachute Regiment. The fighting was very intense with 1 and 4 Troop taking the brunt and at one time the squadron's HQ was in danger of being assaulted. After three hours of intensive firefight the first wave had been beaten off and the enemy had retired. There was a sufficient lull that enabled a handover at 15.00 hrs to the Lincolns. The price of this considerable victory was very high as far as the Germans were concerned, alas for "C" Squadron it had its sad toll with the loss of Sergeant John Collins when his armoured car received a direct hit from a Panzerfäust; Trooper Kenneth Forshaw and Trooper Cyril Baker were killed by shell fire, the wounded included Sergeant B Davenport, L/Sergeant F Turner, L/Corporal R Ellis Troopers T Crabtree, J Harbottle, J Lucas, and J Sherbourne.

From the 7th October as part of Bobforce they then held a ten-mile line stretching either side of their base at Ryckevorsel between Bolk and St Leonard. Although a lot of the patrolling was done on foot the armoured cars were equally involved and they took many prisoners. Like most armoured vehicles the heavy had two exit points. There was one at a lower level just behind the driver's position, the other is on the top of the turret where the two top covers hinge backwards. It was on October 16th that the crew of a Heavy found the disadvantage of these two exits. Whilst out on patrol they were travelling along a narrow road with a water filled ditch running along their left-hand side. The edge of the road had suffered shell damage and as over five tonnes of armoured car started to negotiate the damaged road it side slipped and turned over such that it wedged both of the exits against the banks. Although every effort was made by the rest of the troop it was not possible to save the trapped crew of Corporal Ralph Arran, Troopers Joseph Fairhurst and Harold Nickells.

On the 11th of October, "A" Squadron relieved "C" so that they could have short rest and reorganisation. It was most probably during this reorganisation that Jimmie was brought forward from the Regiment HQ where he had struck up a good relationship with Bill Windsor commonly known to all as "Q" as he escorted him on his deliveries to the various squadrons.

"Q" was one of the few Polar Bears I can remember phoning my father. I can recall one occasion when I answered the ringing phone "Can I talk to Lieutenant Knox?" a voice at the other end asked. Now in my ignorance at sixteen years old I did not appreciate that Lieutenant came before Captain in order of rank. Since like most old soldiers who had seen active service my father had never talked to his children about his involvement in the war. It was only from noticing that on some of his mail that he was addressed as Captain that I had any idea of his previous rank. I just thought that the call was a hoax, yes we had them in the late '50s, so I told the caller politely "No" and replaced the receiver on its cradle. Needless to say in short order the phone rang again. Same question, same answer. My father who was in the kitchen looked at me enquiringly and I said that I thought it was a nuisance call. The phone rang again, my father came forward and I let him answer the phone. He listened obviously to the same question and then I heard his reply. "Hello "Q" good to hear from you. Where are you at the moment?.......". I asked my father to apologise to "Q" for me. Afterwards my Father explained that "Q" had been in the services with him and was now a long-distance lorry driver and as he was in the locality he had given him a call.

At this time Jimmie was commanding a Humber Heavy and these duties continued after he joined "C" Squadron. For the first time he took part in forward searches and patrols keeping a high explosive shell in the breech of his 76 mm gun, arguing that if caught by surprise a loud bang going off might cause the enemy to keep their heads down sufficiently for him to take the initiative.

On 20th October they left for more offensive action with Clarkeforce. Throughout the 25 miles of the advance they led the tanks into action, often having to fight their way against stubborn opposition from enemy infantry, paratroopers and self-propelled guns. They went through Brecht and just north of the town of Wuurstwezel, they reached the main Antwerp to Breda road at Stonebridge. This key bridge was captured intact and was then guarded by the Recce. A three-day lull in the advance at Nieuwmoer enabled "C" Squadron to do some excellent patrolling north east of the village where they directed the artillery on too many targets. In the next ten days they passed through Essen and onto Wouw, inflicting great damage on the enemy. The price of this advance was the lives of Corporal Stanley Hurst, Troopers Arthur Wright and Alfred Murrell,

Rank was no protector from harm for on 26th October the Squadron Leader's car got in the way of shellfire, Major Judge bailed out unharmed but his driver Trooper W Nash was wounded.

The German defence at the Mark Canal was very stubborn and with a lot of open ground to cover a full scale infantry attack was required to beak the line. With the experience of Le Havre the 49th Recce was used to provide a phantom radio network to help coordinate another successful operation.

Apart from a couple of short breaks they had been active since they landed in France four months ago. November gave them the opportunity for a well earned rest and recreational transport was arranged to Antwerp. Buddies Jim Starkey and Donald Hurley took advantage of an excuse to get away and explore Antwerp. Although Antwerp was now in allied hands it was not out of the war. The RAF had command of the skies keeping air attacks at bay but Hitler's Vengence weapons were still flying and on 11th November one found its way to a particular spot in Antwerp killing both friends.

Chapter 12   His Time Has Come

The high temperatures and sun of summer were now getting lost in the dull and rainy days, November weather was coming down over Europe. The Squadron Leader Major Harry Judge together with his second in command Captain K Baker used the stand down period to reassess the disposition of his troops and to fill in the gaps created by the dead and wounded. Jimmie did as he usually did during these times of reshuffle, he hoped, he waited and hoped some more. This time a call came, he had to report to the Squadron Leader. Was it to be what he wanted or another disappointment? After the required salute he was asked to relax and take a seat. The Squadron Leader had some good news for him. He was moving Lieutenant Swindells and told Jimmie that he was to replace him as 3 Troop Leader. At long long last another of Jimmie's ambitions had been fulfilled. Diminished was the sadness of losing his Captaincy at the beginning of the year. He now had his command, two light reconnaissance cars called Cavalier and Champion and two heavy armoured cars Crusader and Covenanter. Eleven men whose lives as well as his own were dependent on his decisions. To each of those there would be mothers and fathers, possibly wives and children however in the heat of battle he would have to place them out of his mind and concentrate on the purpose at hand, the consequences would have to be worried about afterwards. Becoming leader of 3 Troop would mean that he couldn't keep his motor home of the past few months, 4.5 tonnes of steel which had carried Jimmie and his two crew plus all their kit, tools, but most importantly a radio and ammunition. As leader he had to change from a Humber Heavy to the designated Troop Leader's Humber Light. Its steel armour plating was strong enough to stop rifle and light machinegun fire but it was more susceptible to mines and antitank rounds.

His driver Cecil Kirby was a 24 year old who came from a small hamlet in northern Oxfordshire called Twyford Wharf. Its name derived from where the boats operating along the seventy-eight mile long Oxford Canal would stop to load or unload cargoes or to use the local winding hole to turn the boat. The Oxford canal linked the Thames at Oxford with Bedworth where it joined the Coventry Canal and was in its heyday a major commercial route. He lived with his father Frederick, his mother Elizabeth five brothers and four sisters. The family of twelve living in one of the deep honey coloured ironstone houses alongside the road leading to Twyford a nearby village spread along the Banbury road that connected it to the main village in the area of Adderbury. Cecil was a well liked lad that was often seen at the Church of St Mary's in Adderbury.

With the outbreak of war Cecil and his five brothers joined the services. Whilst Cecil had been training to fight in preparation to get to grips with the Germans in North West Europe his younger brother Arthur was with a territorial unit the 8th Battalion of the Royal Fusiliers. Arthur with his unit had fought his way up from the toe of Italy and by February had reached Monte Cassino. This had been the winter stumbling block for the Allies and if the war in Italy was to be successful the Gustav or Winter Line, as it was known by the Allies, had to be broken at Cassino. Arthur Kirby and the 8th Battalion of the Royal Fusiliers were to become an ill fated part of making that breach. In an outflanking move they landed at Anzio where consolidation was the keyword rather than attack. This gave the German commander Kesselring time to build a solid defensive ring around the beachhead from where they had a commanding position. In a dramatic German counter-attack by infantry and tanks on 16th February the 8th Battalion suffered heavy casualties, X Company was reduced to only one officer and 20 men and a similar fate befell that of Y Company who was reduced to merely a single officer and 10 other ranks. It was during this battle that Cecil's twenty year old younger brother Fusilier Arthur Gerald Kirby went missing and later was declared dead.

Whilst Judge was reorganising at Squadron Level Field Marshall Montgomery was regrouping his forces ready to launch the battle for the Rhineland. The 1st Canadian Army extended its front to the salient at Middlelaar south of Nijmegen. The 2nd British Army faced the German bridgehead west of the Rhine. The Polar Bears were allocated to the 12th Corps with the task of advancing on Venlo 35 Miles south of Nijmegen.

On the 7th November orders were received transferring the 49th from the 1st Canadian Army to the 2nd British Army under 12th Corps. Jimmie was in the front line, going into action with the hope that he was going to take the war onto German soil. Before he could get into front line action he had to travel the 120 Km to southern Holland from where operation Chester was to start. On the 14th November they moved off in convoy via Wustweezel, Herenthals, Lommel to a small town situated 16 Km south of Eindhoven. They were fifty kilometres west of their destination near Venlo.

The upcoming operation was intended to clear the Germans from the east bank of the Maas and to take Blerrick on the Dutch side of the river at Venlo. It was going to be a hard struggle this last stretch of land before the Germans would be fighting on home soil. Then the ground lost would be of their Fatherland. The countryside was not in their favour either especially if you add to it the wet weather with almost continuous rain falling onto an already largely waterlogged countryside. There were few roads of any consequence that converged on Blerrick so there was no guessing by the Germans how the Allies were going to approach. With the rain and heavy vehicles it would not be long before the tracks would be turned into mud. With muddy tracks it would become difficult to see the disturbed surface hiding mines.

Having arrived at Borkel new instructions arrived for them to go to Beringe. They proceeded in convoy with "C" Squadron in the lead. On the 19th November they passed over the Zig Canal using a bailey bridge called Cameron Bridge, through the bridgehead held by the 51st (Highland) Division and into the difficult terrain of the front line. Progress in the area was slow due to the presence of mines. Arriving at the outskirts of Beringe "C" Squadron passed on the northern edge and paused just outside Kaumeshoek whilst Lieutenant John Tallack took 7 Troop on foot across country to a small group of houses due east. Once he had ascertained that there was no enemy presence the rest of the Squadron together with two groups of tanks joined them later and formed a tight harbour for the night.

"B" Squadron turned left at Beringe onto Hoogstraat proceeding to In de Hoeven where they Harboured for the night. "A" Squadron turned into Beringe establishing its harbour in the outer suburbs behind the church of Sint Jozefkerk, on Kanaalstraat. The brick-built church in the style of the Amsterdam School was constructed in 1929 on the site of an 1872 pilgrimage chapel in honour of Our Lady of the Sacred Heart. Its tall tower had fallen, quite literally, on the 15th November as part of the retreating Germans destruction of anything that could be used by the advancing Allies to their advantage. The Regimental headquarters set themselves up on the outer fringes of Beringe to the east of the church two hundred metres away from "A". A quick patrol sweep indicated that Beringe was clear although they did suspect that the Germans still had a presence in Panningen two kilometres along Steenstraat to the east.

Following a local area search a suitable property was found to use as their RHQ base. It was into the house at Kanaalstraat 75 on the south side of the road that Lt Col J P F Miles moved and set up his command centre.

Chapter 13   The Peace Baby

The house chosen by Lt Col J P F Miles was owned by Mr Jan Stammen, who like Jimmie was given the same name as his father. Last month on Sunday the 8th October he was taken by the Grüne Polizei in a Nazi razzia and together with 300 other men was transported as a prisoner of war to Watenstedt in the German industrial Ruhr. There he was to work in the manufacture of materials for their armaments industry. He had left behind his wife Nellie and a son named Wiet aged five and an eight year old daughter named Annie. They together with Rika, her 19 year old sister in law were all living at number 75. During periods of bombing and fighting they would retire to the relative safety of their basement, which is where they were when Lt Col J P F Miles arrived.

The front room of the house was set to the right of the front door with a large rectangular front-facing bay and a large window overlooking the side garden and a small orchard of pear, apple and cherry trees. The room was laid out as a dining room and had partitioning doors between it and the room behind that was of a similar size. The rear room was furnished as a less formal sitting area with a similar window having the same aspect to the side as the front room. Lt Col Miles laid out his maps and papers on the table in the front room. With him was his second in command together with the squadron leader of "A" together with his number two. Then the war for them stopped for just a few minutes and in that time the humanitarian side of the attending soldiers came to the fore. Into the room walked a heavily pregnant young lady. There was an obvious language barrier between them but given the girl's predicament, intuition and commonsense played their part. Initially they thought that she wanted to go to the hospital however with the words "Dokter" and "Ya" together with hand gestures she conveyed to them that she was nearly full-term and needed a doctor, not a hospital. Had she been wounded no doubt their medical expertise would have enabled them to help but in the handling of a pregnant woman about to give birth they were out of their depth. With further interpretations of Dutch and English together with more hand signs and with fingers pointing at the map to a place in Panningen the pieces of the puzzle came together. Lt Col Miles was not happy to transport her to the doctor as in her condition the ride could be too rough and promote things. He was also concerned that Panningen was still occupied and he didn't know exactly where the doctor lived. At this point Rika was introduced and agreed to direct them to the doctor's house. With Miles's permission one of the Officers using the CO's jeep took Rika and set out to collect Doctor Smeets.

Panningen was two kilometres, along Kanaalstaat through the village of Everlo and then continuing onto Steenstraat. It was a nerve rendering ride not knowing if they would run into a German patrol, run over a mine or worse. Carefully negotiating the war strewn debris on the road they reached Panningen and then zig-zagged through the streets to the house of Dr Smeets. He knew Nellie and that her condition must be critical at this time and did not hesitate to gather his bag and returned with them to Kanaalstraat 75. They arrived back safely to find that Nellie had been made as comfortable as possible in the next room behind the partitioning doors. With the moans of her ordeal heard by the officers in the front room and with the help of her sister in law she was delivered of a baby girl who she called Ellie. The next day the war moved on but because of the fighting in the area and the risk of mines Nellie was not able to get to the city hall to report her birth. Jan Stammen (Snr), her father, officially registered Ellie's birth as the 25th of November making it her birthday, six days after her actual date of birth that was recorded in the British medical records.

For Nellie and her now three children liberation arrived on that Sunday 19th November and the war moved away.

The Peace Baby

Although circumstances didn't change immediately the atmosphere was friendly and slowly food supplies began to improve. For Jan Stammen (Jnr) in "the hell of Watenstedt " it was life much the same as usual. He and his contemporaries had work and living conditions comparable to concentration and work camps; almost no food, hard labour, cruel treatment, hunger, disease and pests. In January 1945 Watenstedt was bombed and the complex suffered badly. As production was halted Jan was moved to another factory in the area. With the advances made by the allied troops the Industrial Ruhr was surrounded in April and after two weeks the German resistance had crumbled. Late in April a dishevelled, dirty and exhausted Jan started his long walk home. 400 Km which for a normally fit person would take 74 hours, for Jan in his poor physical condition and over war-torn countryside it was going to take him until June to reach home. On the way food was hard to come by, chocolate and cigarettes were perhaps the easier to cadge from allied troops but sometimes it was difficult to convince them that he was Dutch not German. Once in Holland he was fortunate to get a lift in a van the final few kilometres to home.

The bedraggled, unshaven, tired and dirty vagrant that called at Kanalstraat 57 was not recognised by the children but the eyes of Nellie saw through the dirt. It was her Jan, the man she had thought that she may never see again. He was standing before her, home again. After a bath, a shave and having changed into some fresh clean clothes the children recognised their daddy again and Jan, in a wonderful reunion, could hold his wife and children including, for the first time baby Ellie.

After the war they continued to live in Beringe and as one of very few girls of her time Ellie received a decent level of education in the school next door before she was pulled out to have a job as a teacher. She fell in love with and married a teacher in the rebuilt church of Sint Jozefkerk just across the road from where she lived. The newly married couple went to live in Meijel a little town just four kilometres to the east of Beringe where in 1971 they built a house. She developed into a very special lady. She was very smart and spoke four languages fluently. She was very curious, headstrong, caring and had a remarkably dark sense of humour. In 1974 Ellie had her first child, a girl that they called Irene. As was the custom in those days she became 'a stay at home mum', never going back to work. Three years later she had another daughter they named Margot concluding in 1980 with a son they called Joost.

Under her parentage the children grew and matured with Irene and Joost moving to live in Eindhoven, not too far away from the family home. Margot currently lives in Amsterdam and works as a freelance (investigative) journalist for several national news outlets in the Netherlands.

Ellie was a very cheerful lady and remained so even during her hard struggle against breast cancer which finally claimed her in 2003 at the young age of 56. She went quietly in the night just like she came into the world.

Interestingly Dr Smeets who had attended Nellie in 1944 had a son who went on to become a dentist. The son also remained in the area and it was to him that Ellie and her family went for treatment.

Because it is an important example of how in the midst of destruction people decide to help the helpless Margot wishes to thank those brave soldiers who cared enough and risked their own lives to fetch a doctor so that Ellie lived, which in turn is the reason that she exists.

Ellie Stammen in School at the Age of Eleven

The Stammen Family in 1950
Wiet - Nellie - Ellie - Jan - Annie

Chapter 14   The Fight Continues

Another dawn, another day. The sun crept over the horizon its face hidden behind the grey November clouds that threatened to give the war-torn land beneath it another wash. Mother and baby were doing well and early searches by "A" Squadron had indicated that the enemy had withdrawn from Panningen. A more detailed search confirmed the earlier information and Lt Col Miles moved his RHQ to the other side of Beringe harbouring near Everlo at the junction between Steenstraat and Groenstraat. "A" Squadron remained in situ for another night and continued to use number 57 as their headquarters

The various movements of the three Squadrons did not always mean that they had distinct and isolated orders with separate districts to check and clear. Sometimes their movements were like a well choreographed ballet as they quartered and swept and cross-checked areas of known enemy occupation. They would also respond to requests from infantry units who had become bogged down by strong defensive positions. A typical example was when they moved on from Beringe into an area of 500 hectares between "C" Squadron's base of Koningslust and the village of Tongerlo.

The local town's name derived from the two names meaning "Lust of Kings" must surely be a good omen. The building in which they stayed together with the local town was built by Captain de Koning of the Dutch East India Company who made part of his fortune from the slave trade. This area in Helden was his utopia into which he retired in the early nineteenth century. His son Leonard became a priest and founded on the estate in 1846 a new order called "The Brothers of the Third Rule of the Holy Francis". Besides tilling and cultivating the soil they built a home for those with learning difficulties including children. In that home they included a chapel. In 1883 all the property and the surrounding estate was bequeathed to the Catholic Church. By the time Jimmie arrived the fire destroyed building had been rebuilt and the institution had been taken over by monks from the Order of the Brothers of Holy Joseph. They had travelled from a monastery along the river Meuse at a place called Heel. It is not clear from the records if Bacchus juice was dispensed during their presence or not. I would suspect that it was. I would also surmise that those with learning difficulties were also present as there still remains an institution for them in Koningslust today even though the original building no longer stands. The ageing Monks sold off their three farms together with the main building and had a modern well equipped home built on the grounds of one of the farms and now in their retirement, they watch their old-world change about them.

Having spent the night of the 19th on point "C" Squadron then patrolled northwards along Sevenumsedijk where they came upon a German section post. After a short contretemps the post was destroyed killing one and taking nine prisoners of war. On their right flank the Kings Own Yorkshire Light Infantry was being held up by the Germans staunch resistance from a Farm. Lieutenant Hinman of 1 Troop in a masterly and courageous action enabled them to fight their way into the farm taking 2 prisoners and putting another four out of action before handing over to the infantry.

"B" Squadron left In de Hoven adventuring east and onto N277 Middenpeelweg just east of Koningslust where that evening they relieved "C" Squadron. Unfortunately for "B" Squadron "C" Squadron had already attracted serious attention from Self Propelled guns and small arms fire from the nearby woods occupying the local high area. "C" Squadron relieved in more ways than one returned to their harbour of the previous night.

During the night "B" Squadron patrolled into the woods to find that the Germans had retired to occupy other woods southwest of Tongerlo. The next day they moved to the west side of the woods and "A" Squadron came forward on the right meeting some opposition and having to negotiate their way past many mines before they consolidated in the area to the south-east of the woods near Tongerlo. In the meantime "C" Squadron moved east through Koningslust to harbour at the local Cloisters no doubt hoping that the monks would have reserves of Bacchus juice that they would like to share.

During the day of 22 November the 4th Armoured Brigade with whom the Recce had been working went into reserve and the Regiment reverted to Divisional command with instructions to protect the left flank of 56 Brigade as they moved east towards the northwestern edge of Blerick, the object of operation Chester.

As they drove along Breetse Peelweg towards the town of Maasbree they should have been able to see the church spire in the centre of the town, however since it was deemed to give the advancing troops an advantage it was demolished. From Maasbree only three roads of any consequence converge on Venlo from Sevenum, Bong and Blerrick via Rooth and these ran across completely flat and largely waterlogged countryside. By the evening of 22nd November to the great relief of the locals, Maasbree had been liberated. "A" Squadron set up harbour in the south east corner of the town at the south end of Wilhelminalaan, covering the roads to Bong. "B" Squadron harboured half a kilometre north of "A" on Groesweg covering the road to Rooth and six kilometres further on was Blerick. C" Squadron positioned themselves another kilometre further north on Lange Heide at the junction of roads from Massbree, Lange Heide, Korte Heide and Sevenum. They chose to stay that night not far from the junction at house number 3, a farm owned by the

Peeters family. It was with much regret that in trying to hide a Humber Heavy in the barn attached to the house that a misunderstanding between the car and the entry doorway involved a modification of the left-hand side of the doorway.

The news of their success was circulated by the Polar Bear News as this extract from the issue dated 22nd November 1944 shows

> *"In the south east of Holland the British 2nd army have advanced to within 3 miles of the vital Maas bridge at Venlo. They are closing in on the town from the south-west and the west and have liberated the small town of Maasbree."*

Operation Chester was drawing to a close, although some fierce fighting lay ahead that would cause "C" Squadron some heavy casualties. Facing them were the 606th Infantry Division. Although scouting had indicated that they had withdrawn across the Maas they had been replaced by a battle hardened, strong parachute troop rearguard. They were complete with assault guns and the determination to hold the Polar Bears for as long as possible.

Another November day was about to dawn, once again the sun chose to hide behind grey clouds this time trying to prepare to wash away the blood of fighting yet to come. At 05.00 hrs on a wet dark and miserable morning of the 23rd of November numbers 4, 5 and 7 Troops began a cross-country advance on foot. 5 Troop took the road north towards Sevenum. As they moved up they encountered Schumines that caused Cpls F Wilkes, and C McDonald together with Tpr J Harbottle to sustain injuries. They then continued on their way and closed in on the area of De Vorst when they came into contact determined to hold up 5 Troop's advance. The troop Leader made a radio request for assistance for some additional firepower. In response Jimmie was ordered to take his 3 Troop and provide that firepower.

Leading his Troop in a Humber Light called "Champion" with Trooper Cecil Kirby as Driver and L/Corporal Turtle as Machine gunner he was followed by a Humber Heavy called "Covenanter" commanded by Sergeant Eason with Trooper Constable as his gunner. After them came another light called "Cavalier" and bringing up the rear was another Heavy called "Crusader" under the command of L/Corporal Macey with gunner Trooper Thomas and driver Sergeant Wilf Mould. They left the farm turning right on Lange Heide. He paused at the crossroads and checked that the Troop was all present.

The locals had watched as the Germans buried plate looking mines about 300 mm in diameter and 100 mm thick. As far as the Dutch were concerned they were mines, to the Germans they were Tellermines containing 5.5 Kg of explosive with a pressure operated fuse. It was primarily designed as an anti-tank mine as it needed a pressure of 91 Kg to trigger the fuse. It was powerful enough to blast the tracks off a tank or destroy a lightly armoured vehicle,

That morning at the road junction was a gathering of locals all waving and calling out. Jimmie had his radio earphones on and could not hear above the noise of the engine what they were saying. He thought that they were just waving and cheering them on. They were in fact actually calling "Minen" and trying to stop him from driving into a disaster. He gave the instruction to turn right onto Rozendaal and dutifully Kirby obeyed. It was raining, the road had been churned by the passing of retreating tanks and heavy military vehicles, the visibility was poor. Nobody could determine any slight disturbances in the surface of the road ahead. The calls of the locals were now 400 metres behind them, their advice unheeded and then it was too late.

At only 3 tonnes in weight and with just 6 mm thick underbody protection Jimmie's car was not going to survive well against the Tellermine. The blast both lifted and penetrated the underside of the car killing Kirby instantly, injuring Turtle and made the car unserviceable.

For Frederick and Elisabeth Kirby in Twyford Wharf the news of Cecil's death was going to be a second blow after having lost their youngest in February. This would raise fresh fears in their hearts about the risks in which their remaining four boys could be involved in the various theatres of the war.

Although not yet born Steven Spielberg could not direct another as yet unborn Tom Hanks as Captain Miller to enact the spectacular saving of a Private Kirby. However, similar thoughts must have been in the minds of the military for it was not long after Cecil's death had been notified that one of the four remaining serving brothers was discharged. Thankfully for Mr & Mrs Kirby the black cloud of another devastating notification was never to happen.

Jimmie survived with just a cut knee not severe enough to take him out of the fight; the incident shocking as it might have been was not going to stop him. Taking his command seriously, to lead from the front, he grabbed the Bren gun from its mount on "Champion" he then climbed onto the back of the following Heavy and rested the Bren on the turret. He was ready for the fight and ordered them forward.

A kilometre away still on Rozendaal was a house. It had stood on the east side of the road since 1938 just before the war; it was lived in by the family Duijf. They had a five year old boy called Jo. He was given strict instructions to

keep away from the windows since there could be fighting.
Little boys being little boys always do as they are told and

Aerial View in 1944 Showing Positions on 23rd November

Jo was no different. Standing on a chair and looking through the kitchen window he had a good view down Rozendaal towards Jimmie's oncoming convoy of armoured cars. He heard the explosion and saw the pall of smoke drift skywards not realising that that was the end of Kirby's war. He saw a soldier climb onto the back of a big tank like car and watched as they came closer and closer. One hundred metres in front of his window was a road that ran in an easterly direction to Lamerskamp and Zonneveld. The column arrived at the junction and after hesitating they turned right and proceeded down the road right in front of the kitchen window with Jo looking on from inside. He saw the blast, he heard the explosion, he saw the car lift its nose skywards, he saw the gun of the soldier on the back come back and hit him in the face, he saw the soldier fall to the ground, he didn't see him move.

A second car was now out of action and its commander Sergeant Eason was wounded, the driver and gunner escaped unhurt obviously the 10 mm thick underbody armouring on the Heavy stopped the force of the Tellermine's explosive effect. Jimmie was not a pretty sight, the butt of the Bren had come back at him with the full force of the explosion. It had smashed the bridge of his nose and cracked his skull above his right eye. After a cursory examination they placed him on the side of the road to await the burial party.

Sergeant Wilf Mould led the remnants of 3 Troop to link up with the hard pressed 5 Troop and showed a bit more muscle that successfully saw off the resistance. After establishing all was okay with 5 Troop he retraced his route back to the scene of the last incident to see how his colleagues had faired. When he arrived he found Jimmie assigned to the side of the road and he knew what that meant. In early November when Jimmie had taken over the Lead of 3 Troop he had become his Sergeant where as part of his duties he could discuss with him the various options open to him, adding his greater experience to the limited command knowledge of Jimmie. This was Wilf's last opportunity to see Jimmie and say goodbye before he became another statistic on the fatalities list and buried under the soil of a country he fought to liberate. Jimmie lying on the grass verge, his nose smashed and judging by the shape of his forehead over the right eye it appeared that his skull has been fractured. The bleeding had stopped as was to be expected for a chap in his condition. The rich red blood was beginning to turn brown where it had congealed as it had run down his face. His face had also lost its fresh weathered look and had turned to an unhealthy shade of green. Wilf stood there and looked at his Lieutenant who only an hour ago was the same as the rest of them. A family man who longed for his letters from home, from his wife of just five years who would tell him the latest news of his son, their son, the son that he had held so few times and now would do no more. She would tell him about the bright side of her life not worry him about the bombs and devastation all about her. How he would reply telling her that he was safe and that by Christmas it was all going to be over and he would return home to see her, hold her and his son. They were a wartime bride and groom only sharing those snatched precious hours of a few days leave never getting to know each other and for their love to develop into that deeper love that comes with time. That was not to happen, another letter would arrive, not from her beloved Jimmie but from a government clerk, a cold and impersonal letter with all the nice platitudes that are said on such occasions. But no matter how well couched still meant that she would see him no more and what was even worse he would be buried in some foreign field, albeit forever England, he was not to rest under the soil of his beloved England where she and his son could easily visit.

In Wilf's mind he remembered the happy times of fun and laughter as well as those of a more serious nature. Those few short weeks of November after Jimmie had taken over, where he had won his respect as Troop Leader. This innocent and fun loving man who only the other night had shared with him a bottle of the Monk's special. Was he that innocent? Were any of us that innocent? We are here for a cause which we believe to be right, along the way we have been trained, trained how to kill, taught how to survive; it was kill or be killed. All those hours when we were indoctrinated, brainwashed, put it how you will, the result was the same to achieve soldiers that would obey orders without question and in Jimmie's case, as an officer, to issue those orders. To destroy the enemy, the bad guy, the one on the other side who like you had gone through a similar process of indoctrination and believed their cause as equally right as yours. They even most probably prayed to the same God for the safety and success of their cause and their loved ones at home. The memories of this sudden change from a young, bright, fun loving but also a serious soldier to one that had been smashed into a lifeless corpse never to enjoy or be enjoyed by life again passed through his mind. The realisation that when that switch was flicked they became a monster in themselves one that was prepared to do exactly the same to another mother's son as had happened to Jimmie, to be the perpetrator of man's inhumanity to man. Had they become a character they were not proud to admit they had become, was it that that made the old soldiers keep their memories tucked away in the mind never to share?

Wilf bent to touch him on the shoulder as a gesture of a last farewell when he thought that he heard something. Was that natural stomach gasses escaping through his trachea and over his larynx or did Jimmie moan? He crouched beside him his hand reached out to feel his neck, to check for the carotid artery. Was there a pulse; was there any sign of life? His fingers pressed on the neck searching for the artery, for that life meaning sign. Did his fingers deceive him, he tried again, it was there a pulse very feeble and very slow but it was definitely there; Jimmie was hanging in there on the thinnest of threads.

He was in a very bad way, thankfully though he was still alive!

It was Wil's next actions that undoubtedly saved Jimmie's life, for which I will be eternally grateful. He ensured that he got attention from the medics and taken away from that dreaded position on the side of the road awaiting the men with shovels. In their turn the medics saw that he was taken to the Field Surgical Unit attached to the local Casualty Clearing Station where all they could do was to stabilise him and patch him up.

At that time it was unlikely that the field dressing station was operational at 5 Eerselsberg where the locals had earlier that day tried to warn him of mines. It was also questionable if the boy's school on Dorpstraat in Maasbree town centre was functioning as a temporary hospital either. Wherever it was he needed greater medical skills than was available at Maasbree and was made ready for the 175 Km move by ambulance to 8th British General Hospital in Brussels. It was a long and tortuous journey over battle savaged roads with ambulances and the wounded heading the same way as Jimmie and coming in the opposite direction were the bright young faces of their replacements, those men waiting for dead men's shoes. Friday evening the 24th of November saw him still unconsciously ready for what was to happen next.

Cecil Ernest Kirby   Wilfred Mould

Chapter 15   The Recce Fights On

Perhaps Jimmie's days as a fighting soldier were over, the war was not. It was hoped that it would be finished by Christmas but there was still a lot of fight left in the Germans especially as they were now fighting for home soil. The killing and dying were to continue for the Recce. The Squadron pressed forward reached Grubbenvorst on 25th November and the outskirts of Blerick on the same day bringing to a successful conclusion operation Chester but the enemy was still fighting back. Germany was just the other side of the river Maas and on this side there was still some tough opposition to ferret out and destroy.

For the next week various sweeps of the surrounding countryside to the west of Blerick were carried out bringing in a handful of prisoners. Blerick nestled, surrounded on three sides by a bend in the river Maas and was connected to Venlo the last major town in Holland just 3 kilometres from the German border by a bridge, which at that time was still intact since it was being used as a relief passage. The major source of danger was from the enemy artillery.

It was on the night of 28th November when "C" Squadron was relieving the Gloucesters in a small village called Boekend that they found themselves on the pointed end of enemy shelling. They had been out on patrol towards the outskirts of Blerick where they carried out a listening watch to establish if the enemy was still present or if they had left for the other side of the Maas. The listening patrol found it was all quiet so they returned to their base at Boekend and were rather surprised to find that on their way back they were fired upon. They successfully got away without suffering any casualties. The night was still young. After all the brilliant forages forward conducted by Lieutenant Tallack and Sergeant Gatenby, when they had acted as the eyes for our own guns to bring them to bear on specific German targets, the roles were to be reversed for at three o'clock on what was otherwise a quiet night "C" Squadron became the attention of some serious and heavy shelling.

Regretfully a large calibre high explosive shell found the resting area for 7 Troop killing Lieutenant Tallack and Sergeant Gatenby together with Trooper Gore and at the same time wounding five other members of 7 Troop. This was a terrible blow to the squadron as it almost completely took out the whole of 7 Troop.

Late on the 29th, the 51st Highlanders were on the scene to take over allowing the regiment to retire back just behind the lines to Vorst the town they had liberated the week before. It wasn't long before they got new orders. The 49th Division was to proceed north through Nijmegen to relieve the 50th Tyne Tees Division who were currently garrisoning an area known as The Island.

The order to relieve the 61st Recce on The Island was cancelled soon after they had started their move so they halted in a small village called Mill just 20 Km short of Nijmegen. More R&R was on the cards and allowed Major Judge more time to reorganise his squadron after the casualties at Maasbree. The withdrawal of the order to move was because of political troubles brewing in Belgium and there was a possibility that they would follow Jimmie to Brussels to assist the police to maintain public order.

November was also notable for the departure of the Division's GOC "Bubbles" Barker following his promotion to take command of 8th Corps. His farewell message read

> *"It is a great personal regret to me that I have to say goodbye to the Division with which I have been connected for so long. My only hope and ambition has been to help the Division through the campaign with flying colours and I had hoped to see it through to the end.*

> *The record of the Division is a fine*
> *one..........The Polar bear whose butchery*
> *was so kindly mentioned by "Lord Haw*
> *Haw" is a mark of distinction which we can*
> *all be proud to wear. It did not have its*
> *mouth opened without a reason as the*
> *Boche has duly found.......I shall look*
> *forward to seeing you all again in Berlin"*

He wished them many more successes under their new GOC Major-General G.H.A. Macmillan CBE, DSO, MC.

The stay at Mill was comfortable and welcoming whilst they waited for further orders. At that time little did they know of the unpleasant conditions they were going to have to endure in the months ahead.

The most important success of the airborne operations last September was the taking of the bridge at Nijmegen. To hold it they had to establish a bridgehead across the river Waal towards Arnhem that sat on the north bank of the Nider Rijn. The area in between these two rivers was low and flat which proved to be the problem with getting armoured support to the beleaguered troops at what turned out to be a bridge too far. It was eventually confirmed that it would be to this area that they were to be deployed next. The order was reinstated on 12th December and they continued their way through Nijmegen to a little town called Druten on the south side of the winter bund before the river Waal. On the other side of the river was an area known as "The Island".

The Island was an area of 260 square kilometres (26,000 Hectares) of farmland that was just a mere 5 metres above mean sea level. Flat farmland with its patchwork of little fields interspersed with small stands of trees and crisscrossed with drainage ditches. Small villages nestled between the fields with Barns and farmhouses spread across this low lying section of land. Why it was called The

Island I don't know for it ended up over the winter months more like a lake. It was enclosed by two branches of the Rhine. The Rhine splits at the eastern town of Doornenburg with the southern branch called the Waal that flows past Nijmegen and the Neder Rijn that initially flowed to the north before turning west past Arnhem where it flowed in front of the only high ground of the area which was still under German control.

Just after they arrived in Druten they heard the news of a big German offensive through the Ardennes forest. The German High Command had got it right, the area was not as well reinforced and a large incursion was made as the allies fell back. Hitler's idea to split the allied forces became a likely possibility. However, that was without the determination of Maj. Gen. Walter E. Lauer at Elsenborn Ridge where, mainly defended by unseasoned troops, the German advance failed. There was also, perhaps the more credited battle at another important crossroad in the town of Bastogne which was completely surrounded. When Brigadier General Anthony McAuliffe was asked to surrender by von Lüttwitz he made a simple and memorable reply

> *To the German Commander.*
> *NUTS!*
> *The American Commander*

The early anticipation of the war being over by Christmas was not fulfilled; the Battle of the Bulge showed that there was still some fight left in the Boche. A few more months of fighting lay ahead taking the war on to the other side of Christmas. On their arrival at Druten as they took over the positions vacated by the 61st they were welcomed by Lord Haw Haw and his female counterpart Mary of Arnhem in their broadcasts. They told them that the Polar Bear Butchers would be annihilated during the festive season. The 49th had heard it all before and continued to take up the positions vacated by the 61st. One of these positions was on the riverside of the winter bund and was dubbed 4 Post. 4 Post was a brick factory situated almost on the banks of the river. Between the river and the winter bund was an open area 400 metres deep which when they arrived had already been flooded. Access to 4 Post was by boat not only for the troops but also for their supplies. Since the building was in open view to the opposite and enemy occupied side of the river caution had to be used so boat visits could only be done after dark. Christmas was soon upon them and it saw "C" Squadron's HQ residing appropriately for the season in a nunnery in Puiflijk whilst two troops shared the doubtful privilege of spending time at 4 Post. On Christmas Eve it was 2 and 4 Troop's turn at 4 Post. The weather was somewhat colder the usually expected daytime temperatures of $+3^0$C were left behind as the temperature dropped to -1.6^0C and with the clear nights it fell even further. Ice would form over the shallow waters along the edges of the flooded fields. With a hazy cloud cover the waxing gibbous moon whose face would be full in four days time was providing an eerie lightness across the waterlogged landscape.

This was the first Christmas of liberation for the nuns and they prepared special Christmas presents for those soldiers at 4 Post. On Christmas Eve the squadron leader Major Harry Judge together with Captain Webb, the Squadron Rear Link Officer, rowed out across the four hundred metres of freezing waters to the brick factory of 4 Post. They were playing Father Christmas as they took with them not only season's greetings but also the gifts from the nuns both of which were warmly welcomed by the eleven occupants. On leaving the factory the visitors were watched as they rowed away to their warm and comfortable billet by Lieutenant Cox of 4 Troop and Lieutenant Sutton of 2 Troop. As fortune would have it they delayed returning inside instead remained where they were admiring the face of the old man in the moon. Whether it was the movement or a sudden glint of moonlight off a helmet that attracted their attention is immaterial for approaching them, not more than 30 metres away was a fourteen strong German patrol. They had crossed the Waal and were investigating the area to establish what buildings were occupied. As a special Christmas present they were greeted by eleven Bren guns each sending their own stream of gifts. This was not appreciated by the patrol who all retired quicker than they arrived. The following morning investigation showed that they had left a miscellaneous collection of equipment and any injured or dead were taken back with them.

The morning of Christmas Day was celebrated by a memorial service for all the casualties that had been suffered by the squadron and sadly this included the burial of Corporal Kenneth Bond who died the previous day when his armoured car turned over. The Catering Corps did a splendid job of preparing the festive meal which was shared with the nuns. The day was rounded off with a musical evening courtesy of the visiting Recce Corps Band.

The colder than usual winter was aggravated for the occupied Dutch by the total prohibition of the use of electricity. Food was also in short supply making it a cold and hungry winter. In the recently liberated areas food supplies were starting to trickle through and this encouraged those eastern living Dutch who were fit and able to travel to go to the west to get food, even so over 20,000 civilians died of hunger.

The area of "C" Squadron's responsibility along the Waal was between Puiflijk and Leeuwen. It meant that they were back to the early days in France when they were acting as infantry, there was little reconnaissance required or possible. Foot or even boat patrols would seek to find which towns were occupied. This meant that there were a number of firefight skirmishes but a lot of the time they were in static positions

When they arrived at The Island a lot of it was already flooded and it was in the hands of the Germans to flood even more. It wasn't quite no man's land there were some towns and villages occupied with protection provided by the artillery on the higher ground to the north of the Nider Rhine. The area was very easy to flood and even in the dry summertime it was covered by a multiplicity of drainage dykes. There were to be no major movements over the winter months it was to be mostly static listening and watching. Firefights were more frequent as patrols from either side would cross swords as they endeavoured to find out the enemy's strength and disposition. Villages like Dodewaard on the north side of the Waal were to be found ruined by shells and gutted by fire. The receding troops had ransacked and pillaged what had remained and a few miserable cattle were left to their own devices to survive. The bloated bodies of those animals that didn't make it for one reason or another lay floating and rotting in the dykes and waterlogged fields. The town of Opheusden was occupied by the Germans and was in the protective range of their artillery. On their left was the fortified village of Ochten. Then there was Eldikschenhoek where patrols found more of the enemy entrenched, a firefight ensued without any success by either side except each knew they were there. In extraditing themselves Sgt Ridgeway bravely laid down a protective screen to enable the patrol to escape unharmed and for his efforts was awarded the Military Medal. On another occasion Captain Baker together with Tpr Chevinsky were not so lucky both being wounded and taken prisoner. Regrettably Tpr Chevinsky was to succumb to his injuries later whilst being attended to in Apeldoorn hospital.

It was also whilst on The Island that the Squadron Leader Major Harry Judge won his Military Cross. A large number of Germans were spotted advancing down a railway line. Judge engaged them immediately and the Germans took refuge in a nearby farmhouse. Although he realised that he was outnumbered he took the initiative of surprise and pressed home his attack. Taking a small group of men with him they crossed 500 metres of ice packed open ground to reach the farmhouse and forced the Germans to surrender. His citation approved by Montgomery commended his initiative, personal qualities of leadership and grip in achieving success regardless of the hazards of which one was the almost impossible terrain.

January arrived and the weather got even worse with snow and lowering temperatures adding to the misery. Snow over thin ice became a problem as did compacted snow into a minor moonscape of peaks and troughs that could easily upset the most surefooted. Nothing could be worse than when on patrol after being tempted to stand on virgin snow to find that it was covering thin ice and waist deep ice cold water hid below.

January slipped into February and positions continued to be frozen in more ways than one. With the onset of March and with the hint of spring in the air thoughts began to turn to their next mission the crossing of the Ijssel and the advance into Arnhem seven months after the ill-fated attempt by the Paras. Would their long stay in static positions have taken the edge off their ability as Recce?

Chapter 16   Only a Dented Head

Another miserable dawn gradually changed a dark Friday morning in Holland's Limburg region, as it happened it sharpened the contrasts of the greys into buildings and vehicles. Patiently waiting in the expanding daylight was a drab green/grey Austin K2/Y heavy duty military ambulance. On all sides and the top was the white disc in which was painted a red cross of St George. These clear markings were to give it protection from enemy attack for the canvas painted sides would offer no other protection. From inside the building came two orderlies bearing a stretcher and they loaded it into the back of the ambulance. A further three stretchers were brought out, each stretcher holding a war ravaged broken body of a soldier. One of the stretchers held a young soldier who had been added to casualty list 1616, his head was fully swaddled in bandages. Would any of the four who have been carefully placed into the back of the ambulance have injuries that were worse than their bodies were capable of restoring? Would they succumb to the ordeal before reaching Blighty and like some of their comrades be buried in a foreign field? If so, sadly it would not be in the region of their penultimate battle but another cemetery just a bit closer to home where they lost their final battle for life.

The driver and an orderly climbed into the front of the K2/Y, closed the canvas doors beside them and settled down for the long drive. There was the whine of the starter motor then the six-cylinder three and a half litre engine burst into life. A slight noise was heard as the non-synchromesh first gear was engaged and then the three and a half tonnes moved off on a 175 Km journey to British General Hospital number 8. The ambulance would not reach its top speed of 50 mph since it wasn't to be a race against time instead it was to be as comfortable a drive as the suspension and the roads would permit.

It had been only nine weeks earlier that Jimmie had passed through Brussels on his way to liberate Herenhout. The return route was not the same one on which he had travelled out but a shorter one. Hopefully he would be in Brussels by that evening but it was not the same Brussels that he had passed through in September many things had changed and were changing as he lay unconscious in the back.

After 5 years of German occupation Brussels was liberated with special celebrations on 4th September when Piron, who had taken his Brigade out of "C" Squadron in Porthcawl, proudly, as De Gaulle had done in Paris, led his Brigade in a parade through the city centre announcing to all that occupation was over and Belgium was a free nation once again.

With King Leopold III of Belgium still held under house arrest in Germany after surrendering with his army in 1939 it was constitutionally necessary to have a Regent if Belgium was to function as a country again. The Belgium government turned to Prince Charles, Count of Flanders and appointed him as Prince Regent. This enabled the government in exile to become a functioning government of national unity under Hubert Pierlot.

At the beginning of November the last of the German forces in Belgium surrender at a little town on the coast just north of Zeebrugge called Knokke. Herbert Pierlot and his government started to bring the country back to some form of normality out of the chaos of war. One of their early actions was to remove the privileges enjoyed by collaborationist organisations whilst at the same time they reinforced their October request that all resistance groups should hand in their weapons. The Belgium resistance movement was not a single organisation instead there were many and varied Belgium resistance groups divided by region and political beliefs and included men and women from both the Walloon and Flemish parts of the country. The government's main concern was that the resistance would degenerate into armed political militias which could threaten the country's stability. In a tough stance the government even threatened to search homes for weapons they believe had not been handed in. Needless to say this threat provoked significant anger among resistance members some of whom had hoped to continue fighting alongside the Allies. The government's concerns were justified when on the 25th November resistance groups demonstrated in parliament demanding official recognition. The matter escalated and believing that they were trying to make a left wing coup d'état British troops were used to help control the demonstration. Unfortunately shots were fired and forty-five demonstrators were wounded.

Concerns were expressed about the possible further escalation and that additional troops should be brought in to help control the situation. It was for this reason that the 49th Recce was held back at Mill. Fortunately the situation was defused and an attempt by the resistance to enter into politics as a formal party called Belgium Democratic Union failed to attract sufficient interest. Other groups went on to form the Foundation Armée Secrète which continues to fund historical research of the resistance as well as providing assistance for its members.

The decision was taken that the 49th Recce was not required and they were ordered to continue on to The Island.

In the afternoon of 24th November the ambulance arrived on the outskirts of Brussels. The driver negotiated his way through the narrow cobbled streets where the engine and exhaust notes echoed off the buildings on either side. He wound his way towards the former twelfth century leper colony area of Marolles in the town centre. He was searching for Rue Haute and the building that housed the second oldest hospital in Belgium. The building a 1921 purpose hospital of brick construction with three stories housed the 8th British General Hospital (BGH) and was capable of taking up to 1000 patients.

The 8th BGH had followed the fighting, albeit at a distance from Lesneven in Brittany in the early days of 1940 through Rennes and then to Port Tewfik situated at the southern end of the Suez Canal followed by a move to Alexandria. They then followed the invasion forces to Taranto in Southern Italy followed up the leg to Caserta outside Naples. After the D-day landings they found themselves once more following our victorious army in Northern Europe. Setting up in Bayeux in August before they moved camp again in mid September to Brussels to arrive shortly after the town was liberated. They occupied the building that is now part of the St Pierre University Hospital complex.

The ambulance turned into rue Haute and then did the tight turn through the narrow double arched entrance into the hospital. One by one the four stretchers were taken carefully out of the rear of the ambulance and into a waiting bed with Jimmie ending up in a surgical ward. His wounds were carefully checked for any infection and re-bandaged ready for the surgeon's inspection the following morning. The weather the next day did not concern Jimmie for he was still unconscious and remained so during his examination. Apart from a minor cut on his knee caused in the first incident the more serious and life threatening injury was caused in the second incident by the butt of the Bren gun that he had rested on the turret top ready for immediate use. The force of the mine exploding under the armoured car brought the butt and Jimmies head together. The butt hit him in the face, smashed his nose and cracked his skull on his right forehead just above and without damage to the eye. It was this injury that Jimmie always referred to as his **"dented head"** grossly underestimating the trauma that had happened. During the time available to them at the field dressing station in

Maasbree they had just cleaned and bandaged the injury to his knee. They also managed to clean his head wounds but the more serious damage to his head needed the expertise of specialist surgeons. The examination in Brussels concluded that they should reset his nose and make that part of his face good but there was still severe swelling and the cranial fracture needed special plates to be made in order to hold the pieces of his skull together whilst it healed. Experience and timewise it was not something that could be done easily at the 8th BRG so it was recommended that after the nose work he should be sent to the specialist head hospital in Oxford where they had the time, experience and all the facilities required.

By the 28th of November the Port of Antwerp had been declared safe and open to shipping. The use of Antwerp was most welcomed since it shortened the road supply route by 500 Km although it did increase the shipping time because of the additional 120 Km at sea. The saving on fuel, vehicles and personnel involved were all plusses not to be ignored. It was also a godsend to Jimmie since it would save him that 500 Km of bouncing around in the back of an ambulance. On the 3rd December a boat was available and Jimmie was placed once again, together with three others in the back of an ambulance and taken the sixty kilometres to the waiting hospital ship moored in the docks at Antwerp.

By now Jimmie's last letter had arrived at Belvedere. His letters were a welcome relief from her continual worry. She could hear his voice as she read through the lines written in his flowing script. Sometimes the letters were short when he was grabbing those short hours in the evening between movements. At other times when he was standing down for a rest they were much longer. Without managing to disclose his whereabouts he told her about the good things that he had seen and places he had been through where the damage of war had not wreaked devastation on the autumnal prettiness of the villages dotted throughout the countryside. In every letter he always assured her that he was safe and of his love for her. In return her letters told him all about his two year old son and how he was now fully mobile and getting into all sorts of mischief. She described to him almost everything that they had been up to, to bring her home life to be as real to him as she could make it. So that he could whilst reading the letters partake in the pleasures that she had experienced. She too also ended her letters assuring him that they were all safe and well, sending her love and asking him to take extra care of himself.

Then just before Christmas a buff coloured envelope arrived. It lay on the floor just inside the letterbox face down. She had heard of these letters. Nancy stood over it and looked down. If it was addressed to Mr A G Parsons it would be bringing bad news of her brother Bert. Bert she knew was with the Dorsets in North East India or perhaps now even Burma. He would be fighting the Japanese, the weather and the ever present risk of malaria as well as eating enough curry to put him off it for the rest of his life. He was with the Dorsets as a "walky-talky" soldier carrying on his back the foot soldiers equivalent to what Jimmie had in his armoured car. In April 1944 he had been engaged in the battle of Kohima and in the final and successful battle for the Bungalow lost his best friend who fell in the first wave. If on the other hand it had her name on the front it was bad news about her Jimmie, either way it was bad news for the family. She bent down and picked it up, turned it over to look at the address selfishly hoping that it had been wrongly delivered. It hadn't. It had her married name boldly printed on the front, Mrs J.E.Knox. She walked into the room at the back of the shop and sat down before her legs let her down. She was shaking, all the colour had drained from her face, she just felt numb, was this actually happening to her? This is the one envelope that every wife and mother hated receiving and now she was holding it in her hand. She turned it over and quietly and deliberately slid her forefinger under the edge where the flap was partially sealed. The envelope tore as she moved her finger along the top edge. Her shaking fingers withdrew the letter and opened it out laying it flat on her lap. The print was not clear; the tears welling up and collecting along her bottom eyelid were distorting the print. She took a handkerchief and dabbed her eyes, the print came into focus and she started to read. The word she expected to find wasn't there instead she read 'wounded'. She had to read the sentence again, the word didn't change. Jimmie wasn't dead. Jimmie was alive. Jimmie was wounded, just wounded, not dead. The relief flowed through her and she just collapsed into tears.

Her mother came into the room and seeing her daughter in distress together with the letter on her lap understood, feeling that sudden pang in her own heart. She put two and two together and like the first thoughts of her daughter they were wrong. She sat beside Nancy and put her arms about her to console her. It was only when Nancy said that he was just wounded not dead that her mother understood that the tears were ones of relief, not sorrow.

A cup of strong sweet tea was made and slowly Nancy began to calm, the tears became sobs and the sobs reduced in frequency until gone. It was then that she realised that whilst she had been told of Jimmie's condition because she was listed as next of kin but James and Roberta, Jimmie's parents, would still be oblivious to his circumstances. She had to write to them, she must write to them. She knew nothing more than the news contained in that buff envelope. In her immature schoolgirlish handwriting she started to write composing her lines using much the same language as the official, ending that when she knew more she would let them know.

It was during the sea crossing that Jimmie came round albeit for a short time. He recalled being in an open space where there were lots of pipes. He then drifted back into his unconscious world again and the boat sailed on. It had an uneventful and safe crossing entering the Thames estuary just after high water and moored at Tilbury. An ambulance train waited at the nearby platform. Like the road ambulances it had the white disc inset with the red St. Georges cross painted on its roof and sides again like its road vehicle equivalent trusting that it will give it some protection from attack. At that time in the war marauding enemy aircraft were almost nonexistent but there were still the occasional small bombing raids happening over London and these did not distinguish vehicles or buildings displaying the Red Cross. The biggest threat was from the vengeance weapons of the V1 announced by the easily recognised sound of its Argus Pulse Jet engine or the sudden crump of the unannounced exploding V2.

With all aboard the train started to move. As the link between each additional carriage took up the strain there was a jolt then as the load became uniform the train edged its way from the platform heading towards its destination of Fenchurch Street station in central London. Slowly the speed increased and by the time they had reached Grays the clickety-clack of the bogies passing over the joins between the rails were beating out a steady rhythm. Little did Jimmie know or for that matter his wife who was occupying herself preparing the shop for the next day's trade that as the train pressed on along the north side of the Thames past Rainham they were within three and a half kilometres of one another. As the locomotive started to reduce speed as it approached the end of its journey the carriages nudged up against each other adding another little bump to the journey. At Fenchurch Street it was all change and another ambulance ride across the bomb damaged streets of London. The driver weaving his way past hollow shells of buildings charred black, the result of an incendiary bomb attack. Eventually they arrived at Paddington Station. The Great Western Railway operated the West Country route to Bristol with a branch off at Reading that would take him to Oxford. The train this time was not a hospital train per se having just one carriage modified to take stretchers. It is unlikely that Jimmie knew anything about his journey out of London and through the unspoilt green countryside of Berkshire and Oxfordshire. The clickety-clack of the bogies over the joins remained the same although on this journey they were a lot more frequent. The train skirted around Windsor where the King and Queen had spent most of the war and out into the patchwork quilt of the countryside. The smoke from the locomotive's funnel being left behind and then drifting across the fields and little villages its aroma of burnt coal and steam letting them know it had passed. At Reading it stopped to let those that wanted to change to the local and suburban routes disembark. The train left the station and click-clacked its way to Didcot where it slowed, then clattered over the points as it took the spur off towards Jimmie's destination of Oxford passing through quaint villages with names like Appleford and Radley. The familiar bumping of the carriages indicated that the train was slowing. It clattered slowly over the Thames and to their right appeared the sleepy spire of Christ Church Cathedral, and the huge dome of the Bodleian Library, Oxford awaited its new arrival.

Nestling among the sleepy spires of the ancient academic city of Oxford was the comparatively young college for women called St Hugh's. Founded in 1886 by Elizabeth Wordsworth, the great-niece of the poet William, using the money left to her by her father a Bishop of Lincoln. She named it after one of his 12th Century predecessors Hugh of Avalon. Her intention was to enable poorer women to gain an Oxford education. However, Hitler intervened in this endeavour. The war made its imposition on the college, in October 1939 it was requisitioned for the duration by Sir Hugh Cairns assisted by Richie Russel. They turned it into a major centre for head and spinal injuries. Hugh Cairns was an eminent neurosurgeon whose techniques included the use of Penicillin for the first time in England and working at St Hughes he brought the mortality rates down to 10% of what they were in the First World War.

The women undergraduates were moved to other accommodation left vacant by the male undergraduates that joined the services. In 1940 the wonderful lawns and gardens at the rear of the house were used to build one-storied buildings of brick and concrete which were called "ad hoc hutted units" by Whitehall. They were connected together and to the main college by brick corridors. (These buildings remained until the summer of 1952.) The six wards grouped in pairs and suitable to accommodate 300 beds as well as occupational therapy units were erected in the garden. Two wards running east and west were built on the main lawn where the tennis courts had been, two running north and south and reaching to within four metres of the library were built on the Ansell piece and another two also running north and south on the northern half of the Whitehead piece. The design was stairless to make it easy for recuperating patients to move around easily.

At Cowley near Oxford was the Morris car production facility run by Lord Nuffield. It was the metal handling facilities and expertise of the company that was readily adopted by Sir Hugh Cairns and his team to produce special tantalous metal plates, they were implanted into the skull to hold the fragments in position while the bones knitted together as the damaged skull repaired itself.

Travelling north on the Banbury road two and a quarter kilometres from the station the ambulance turned left into St Margaret's Road and then almost immediately left again into the former ladies college of St Hughes. Jimmie was going to be in good hands.

On his arrival he was taken to the officer's ward which was situated on the ground floor at the rear of the building that looked out onto the newly built brick wards and what was left of the lawns and flower beds with the occasional benches occupied by appreciative patients and their visitors.

It had now been two weeks since his injury and although treatment had been given in Belgium time is now pressing to get the damaged head together. The swelling had gone down sufficiently for measurements to be taken and sent to the trained workers at Cowley to make his personalised tantalous plate. On receipt of the plate from Cowley it was offered up to Jimmie's skull to check that it was the fit required by the surgeon and once all was okay the operation went ahead. Christmas passed in a daze for Jimmie and as a special New Years gift he had his operation with the plate being successfully fitted. By the 3rd of January he was recovering well. The sad thing for Jimmie was that on his records he had been designated as medical category D which meant that he was now unfit for any form of military service. Although time will show if this was going to be a temporary measure. It did mean that as things stand not only were his days as a fighting soldier over but possibly his days in the services as well. He had to change his uniform from Army Khaki to the Hospital Blue uniform with a white muslin Mrs Mopp cap. The essential cap that had to be worn by all head patients to protect the injury whilst letting it recover and his hair to re-grow.

After that first bombshell of a letter there was nothing from the government, nothing from Jimmie either. Nancy had no knowledge of where Jimmie was or how badly he was injured. The news from the front was occupied by the latest German offensive in the Belgium Ardennes. Was Jimmie there, had he now become a prisoner of war? Would the Germans look after him properly, after all, she was lead to believe they were all monsters? In her mind she could conjure up many horrible scenarios. The other wives she had talked to in the shop who had husbands and boyfriends that were wounded told her that once her man was back home he would write. Whilst initially this was some comfort as time went by and no letter arrived with the address in Jimmie's hand the more she worried. Christmas 1944 was a sad time in Raynes Park and Belvedere. The world of two year old Peter was not to be invaded by the sad news that his daddy was hurt. Peter's expectations were low as far as Christmas presents were concerned so the special treats all ready for unwrapping on the 25th kept him happy and amused. Nancy's New Years Day was welcomed with wet eyes. It was now over five weeks since he had been injured and nearly a month since that letter arrived; surely if he hasn't been involved in the new offensive then he must be back in the UK but where was his letter. The only glimmer of hope was the fact that another buff envelope has not arrived informing her that he was either a Prisoner of War or had died of his injuries. This glimmer was tested and shaken by every sight of the postman until his latest delivery had been checked.

Nancy would stand and wait in the shop each morning for the postman with each day being a mixture of relief and sadness. Then one day in the middle of January a letter in that oh so familiar handwriting arrived. She looked at the name on the front, it was to her Nancy, not Mrs Knox, the handwriting was definitely his, although a little shaky, what was more there was a British stamp in the top right-hand corner. He was alive, he was home, somewhere in the UK. An excitedly shaking hand tore open the envelope and pulled out the letter. She looked at the end and there it was "Love Jimmie" the tears came in floods, tears of absolute relief. Peter came in and saw her crying and asked why; to which she told him that she had just received a late Christmas present, the best present ever.

Back in Oxford Jimmie's progress was satisfactory for his injury. In general the average stay at St Hughes was two months for Jimmie it was going to be considerably longer.

His first sick period was not due to end until 28th February at which time it was to be reviewed.

Letters to and from Nancy and his parents were a welcome relief from the tensions of those earlier months of silence. Although he was not allowed out at the moment he did get permission for Nancy to visit him. By some means best known to him he managed to get her a travel permit. It would be a long day for Nancy but excitement enabled her to be awake in time to catch the early train. Jimmie had sent a comprehensive set of instructions of where to change and which train to catch. For Nancy this was a massive trip into a big new world. She was surprised at the bomb damage that the docks area had suffered. She was aware of local bomb damage in Belvedere as one night a stick of bombs had destroyed all the houses on one side of Picardy Street but London was of another order. The train having paused on the bridge over the River Thames slowly started to move again and clattered across several points as it was funnelled into the appropriate platform.

The station emptied the passengers onto a busy London street. Nancy was surprised at the number of pedestrians that were about although a lot of them both the men and women were in a uniform of one description or another. The amount of local bomb damage was not as great as she had witnessed as the train passed through the dock area and she was surprised that some buildings appeared to be completely unscathed. She set out walking towards Southwark Bridge looking for the bus stop of the number 18 for Kings Cross Station. She was struggling, confused by the size of the road, the amount of traffic and the number of busses all with different numbers and destinations a far cry from the one trolley bus that stopped outside her father's shop. She must have had the lost look on her face because a mature gentleman paused and asked her if that was the case. With his helpful instructions in her mind she set off across the road and turning left once there she found a stop for the number 18. It wasn't long before a number eighteen arrived and she stepped onto the platform at the rear and headed inside to take a seat on the lower deck just after the bench type seats next to the entrance. The small diamond aperture in the mesh covering the windows enabled her to get a clearer view of the buildings as they passed. The ticket collector, a woman who had taken over a man's job whilst they were at the front, peeled off a ticket from her rack, then there was the familiar ding of the bell as she punched the ticket with the destination of the fare stage for Kings Cross. It wasn't long before they drove past St Pauls and Nancy was in awe with the size and magnificence of the building. It was surrounded by buildings that had suffered in the blitz of 1940 and were now suffering again from the mini blitz of 1944. The damage was obviously from the most recent raids on the night of the 21st 22nd January when 400 aircraft, flying in two waves, dropped 268 tons of high explosive bombs and thousands of incendiaries on south east England and London. Westminster, the Houses of Parliament, Parliament Square and Westminster Hall, had all taken their share of the latest raid. So had the Embankment, Westminster Bridge, New Scotland Yard (Canon Row) and parts of Pimlico all hit by incendiaries. Another raid followed on the 28th when the Surrey docks were firebombed. Yet there was St Pauls in the first light of a winters morning in all its majesty, unscathed, standing there defiantly amidst all that destruction. How, she thought, could people live and work in these conditions not knowing what the next night might bring.

On another matter her curiosity got the better of her, whilst she understood that the mesh on the windows was to protect the passengers from splintering glass she did not know why the front parts of the bus's mudguards were painted white. When the conductress next passed by she asked her and was told that in the blackout it helped the drivers to determine where the outsides of the oncoming busses were. The conductress also added that if she was to look at the back of the bus she would see that on some of them there was a painted white circle. This she explained was painted on busses that shared routes with the trolley busses the idea being that if a following trolley bus driver saw the white circle he knew that it was safe for him to overtake without the risk of dewirement of the overhead power supply poles.

Whether it was for her benefit or not the call went out "Charing Cross Station" and just afterwards the two great brick built arched train sheds with its central 34-metre high clock and bell tower that held treble, tenor and bass bells that alone weighed 1.47 tonnes came into view. It was the London terminal for the LNER railway serving the east coast to Scotland and boasted the great Flying Scotsman service to Edinburgh. The most famous of these was Mallard, which achieved the world speed record for steam locomotives at 126 miles per hour just before the war in 1938. Now it was doing a terrific service moving troops to and from the North European war zone. But it was Paddington Station the London terminus for the Great Western railway that she wanted as it served her destination of Oxford. A short walk along the Marylebone Road brought her to another huge station with the roof over the train shed filling with steam and smoke from the locomotives standing at the platforms. A kindly station porter gave her directions to the platform she needed and off she went to find a seat in a "Ladies Only" section. A whistle blew, a green flag was waved and then there was the powerful snort from the locomotive as it took up the strain of the coaches. Each one causing a ripple of motion down the train's length as each carriage joined with the one in front on its way west.

The crowded suburbs of West London with their vegetable patch back gardens together with a tin bath hanging on the wall outside the kitchen door passed by. She noted that not every house had one; perhaps they had an internal bathroom as she had at Belvedere or perhaps they were using them as a type of Morison shelter to protect a child or baby. Sometimes in back gardens or on common land by the houses would be a grassed mound covering an

Anderson shelter. On the left hand side the houses started to become fewer and soon the countryside replaced them. It was a bleak view she had of the countryside hidden in the early mists but the farmer, male or female she could not determine, was out with his horses and ploughs turning the soil ready for the planting of his next crops. As the train thundered past Slough she could make out the walls and towers of Windsor Castle outlined against the dawn sky where the King and his family were ensconced. The tracks snaked on with the train pausing at Reading to let passengers alight and new ones join and then chugged on to repeat it again at Didcot. All the time the dawn was turning into day with the day becoming more cheerful echoing the feeling in her heart as she got closer to her Jimmie. Just after Didcot the line branched off towards Oxford passing through the same stations with quaint sounding names of Appleford and Radley. It then started to slow and in front she could start to make out the spires and domes of the Universities of Oxford. Nancy took from her pocket Jimmie's letter that contained the instructions about which bus to take and where to get off. She read it;

'you will need to cross over the footbridge to the other platform and then make your way out into the street. Outside the station a number of busses stop they are similar to the ones that you know from home except they were coloured red and dark maroon with pale green relief. Take the number 2 bus to Kidlington and get off at the St Margaret's Road stop; it only takes a few minutes. When you get off the bus you will have to walk back to the hospital which is on the corner of the first turning, St Margaret's Road.'

The pace of the train got slower and as it rumbled over the bridge crossing the River Thames she noticed how unscathed the area was a marked change from where she had left just a couple of hours ago. There was a mini bumping of carriages as the train pulled into Oxford station and then it came to a standstill.

She followed the crowd over the footbridge to the up line platform. She was surprised at how many people had chosen Oxford as their destination. There were a lot of uniforms in the crowd with perhaps the majority RAF blue. As she turned off the platform she could see over the heads of the exiting passengers a red and maroon bus with a pale green line down its side. To one side of the entrance was a white bonnet topping out an army greatcoat. The face was scanning the exiting passengers it looked at her and moved on and then came back and fixed its stare directly at her. The arm of the greatcoat went up and started to wave at the same time the coat started to weave its way through the crowd. The soldier was almost upon her when she recognised the eyes and that tash. It was Jimmie, her Jimmie! She rushed forward not hesitating to think that it could be a stranger and threw her arms around him giving him the biggest bear hug she could. The hug was returned. After a second she began to wonder if she had mistakenly embraced a stranger, after all he had made no mention of meeting her at the station. She leant back and looked at him from the outer edge of her embrace. Although the white bonnet had hidden his distinctive hairline and style, up close she could see that his hair had been shaved away from his forehead and was currently in the process of re-growing, the eyes were unquestioningly his. Any thoughts about the impropriety of public displays of attention vanished. A kiss followed for how long she could not remember but it was long overdue.

Arm in arm they left the station and walked and chatted, she could not hold back, so much to ask. The half a mile to the Randolph Hotel was gobbled up in an array of questions, the next coming before he had a chance to answer the last. How are you? Are you better? Why the white bonnet? When can you come home? They arrived at the Randolph, found themselves a table in the corner of the lounge overlooking Beaumont Street and ordered something to eat and drink.

He told her that he was feeling much better, that the surgeons had done an excellent job and had told him that once all the swelling had gone down he would be left with a small scar on the bridge of his nose and another down the right-hand side of his forehead with the possibility that that one will fade in time. He was due for another assessment on the 1st of March when it was more than likely that he will be re categorised as Category C. A puzzled look from Nancy led him to explain that at the moment he was Category D which meant that he was temporarily unfit for any military service whereas Category C meant that he would be only fit for home service. Nancy felt sorry for him as she knew how much he loved the army and how much of his time he devoted to becoming the best soldier that he could. Inwardly she was pleased that he would not be in the front line risking his life for King and various countries that were only names on a map to her and then not coloured pink. Although the average stay time at St Hughes was three to four weeks he could not see himself being released just yet and hoped that perhaps he would know more at his next assessment when he also hoped that if his wounds had healed sufficiently he would be released from wearing the protective white bonnet.

The conversation drifted on comfortably between them about Peter and how he had grown and was a lot more mobile now and into all sorts of mischief. "Bert" he asked "any news?" Nancy replied that she had received irregular letters, she guessed from Burma, that told her how he was sick to death with curry for breakfast, curry for lunch and curry for dinner seven days a week and he reasoned they would do it for eight days if they could. Apart from that he is keeping fit and well.

Time had slipped by and the return train was heading towards Oxford. They had an hour left before she had to leave and say goodbye so they went for a stroll around the city centre. As they walked she said how surprised she was that there was so little bomb damage. She had expected all of the country to be bombed like it was at home. In reply Jimmie told her a little story that was favoured at the time. He said that since the RAF had started to bomb Berlin the Luftwaffe had decided to get their own back by bombing important towns over here. He went on to tell her that they used the 1937 edition of the 'Baedeker's Great Britain' tourist guide to select those towns with more than three stars and Oxford, unlike its sister university town of Cambridge, was not on that list. She replied that she didn't realise that Belvedere was a tourist attraction let alone with at least three stars. They wandered along beside the river commenting on how much smaller the Thames was with its banks covered in trees and bushes rather than the industrial backdrop and muddy flats at low tide that she was accustomed to along the towpath from Belvedere to Erith. As they approached the station they heard the whistle of her train as it signalled its imminent appearance at the station.

The Ladies Only compartment was found, Jimmie opened the door and then it was time for a parting hug and kiss before she climbed into the carriage. The familiar theme began with the guard's whistle followed by the waving of green flags before the belch of steam from the locomotive heralded the rippling take-up of the strain by the coaches. Nancy stood at the window and waved goodbye until the white bonnet was visible no more.

Chapter 17   The Polar Bears Fight On

With the ending of winter and the coming of spring plans were being made for the move into Arnhem, the town that had evaded the allies the previous September. This attack on Arnhem was to be a two-pronged affair with the Canadian 1st army advancing from Nijmegen to cross the Nider Rhine to the west of Arnhem approximately where the Remnants of the British 1st Parachute Division had escaped in September. The other prong of the attack was to be from the east and this would be undertaken by the 49th Division crossing the Ijssel at Westervoort. In spite of fierce resistance on the 30th March the 7th Canadian Infantry Brigade had reached Emmerik. It fell to 49th Recce to check the area from there forward as far as the railway bridge at Westervoort. They had to establish any enemy positions and other hazards that the infantry would have to deal with in their move forward prior to their attack on Arnhem.

After months of being in static positions on The Island they were only too pleased to get back to the job they volunteered for. "C" Squadron had the task of checking the area beside the river. The squadron was split into two groups one group crossing the Rhine at Emmerich in Germany. They followed the east bank and worked their way up to the area east of the Neder Rhine and then across through Westevoort to the bridge across the Ijssel north of the town. Meanwhile the other group embarked at Nijmegen onto assault landing craft (LCA). They travelled up the Waal and on reaching the junction with the Nider Rhine followed it towards the confluence with the Ijssel. Landing on the east bank before the Ijssel they made their way along on the south side of the winter bund towards the bridge at Westervoort. The area was free of opposing forces however they had left behind mines galore which gave the Squadron the difficult task of marking out safe routes to the river.

Having fulfilled their reconnaissance role they returned to the Island and Druten for exercises to ensure that the new officers and men could enable the squadron to perform in fluid battle conditions as well now as it had through France and Belgium. Then they were ready for their deployment for the assault.

On 13th April 1945 the 49th Recce moved to Zevenaar ready for the assault on Arnhem. This time they were in the vanguard, they had set up a command post and safe routes now it was up to the squaddies and the heavy armour to complete what Major-General John Dutton Frost commanding some 740 men of the British 1st Airborne Division had started in the previous September. The object then was to capture the bridge intact alas in early last October a group of B-26 Marauders of the American 344th Bomber Group destroyed the bridge to stop the Germans from using it to reinforce their troops. With no bridge to aid the 49th's crossing, they used Storm boats and Water Buffalo Amphibian Landing Craft to carry both men and machines across the Ijssel. The battle was preceded by an air raid on Fort Westervoort an important link in the German's Ijssel line of defence. This was followed by a massive artillery stonking on Arnhem and its suburbs. On the night of the 12th/13th a tremendous smoke screen was laid down as the troops of the 49th began their crossing of the river and advance into Arnhem.

The following day whilst the attack on Arnhem was underway it was the Recce's turn to load their Bren carriers and armoured cars into Buffaloes ready for the slow 7 mph crossing of the Ijssel. It is interesting to note that at their crossing point they were halfway between the Normandy beaches, to the west, where they landed last July and Berlin to the east. Some reflected back to the thoughts of the war being over by Christmas and here they were only halfway to Berlin about to join the fight for Arnhem three months into the new year. Would the German resistance continue to remain as steadfast now they were close to the Fatherland making next Christmas the target or would they crumble? Once over the river they sought temporary refuge in one of the straw sheds of the AKU silk factory, then it was forward again, into a heavily damaged and deserted Arnhem.

The town had all appearances of a ghost town when it was finally liberated on 15th April. The troops pushed through and by the following day had reached Schelmseweg on the north of Arnhem and Velp on the east side. On the morning of the 16th April, with Arnhem cleared "A" and "C" Squadrons passed through the bridgehead, moved out to the east. Much to the delight of its residents the Polar Bears arrived at the village of Ellecom. "C" Squadron with "A" on their left flank and "B" on their right headed north heading towards Apeldoorn and were to enjoy a time comparable with their best days in France. Taking 143 prisoners and killing many others.

From her home in a little village called Eerbeek a young lady with a round face and brown wavy hair that just touched her shoulder called Betsy Jansen had heard the artillery barrage during the battle for Arnhem. She knew the live war was getting closer and perhaps liberation was soon to be. Although her village was not garrisoned by the Germans over the past day there had been a lot of German troop movements firstly towards Arnhem and now it was away. She stayed indoors keeping away from the windows for she had heard stories of the callousness of the Germans and did not want to provoke any trouble.

Gerrit Plant, a more mature man slim in stature with brown swept-back hair with a hairline that was beginning to exaggerate his widow's peak also lived in Eerbeek and he was thankful that he had not been caught in the German's net. He too had heard of the failed attempt by a group of the local Resistance to hijack a lorry for one of their schemes to hinder the Germans in the face of the advancing allies. The attempted highjack was made earlier that year in March. An ambush was arranged on the road between Apeldoorn and Arnhem called Oude Arnhemseweg just south of a village called Woeste Hoeve. As the Ambushers waited the sound of a large engine was heard approaching. A young man stepped into the road to stop the vehicle. Unfortunately it was not a heavy lorry but a large BMW carrying the local German chief of security. It was too late the trap was sprung and the security chief ended up dead. In retaliation the Germans took 173 male occupants of the local prison to the spot on the road where the ambush took place and shot them.

Late on the morning of the 16th April the vehicles and troops on the road through her village were that of the 49th Recce. Eerbeek was liberated. Betsy put on her best shift skirt and ruche sleeve top, calf-high socks, for there were no delights as stockings available, and shoes then went out into the village to welcome the liberators. Meanwhile a few houses away Gerrit put on his jacket, waistcoat, collar and tie and also went into the streets to welcome the liberators. The two met as they scrambled onto the front of a stationary Carrier, Betsy with folded arms and Gerrit more relaxed with his hands on his legs had their photo taken for posterity as they hoped that liberation only needs to happen once in a lifetime.

Loenen, the next village to be liberated was just a few kilometres along the road. It was on a junction of four roads Beekbergerweg, Hoofdtweg both leading to Apeldoorn and Groenendaalseweg linking to Arnhem and Eerbeekseweg. They would be using that road to enter Loenen. Was there to be a German defensive position along this road or perhaps in Loenen itself? After lunch Number 3 Troop took the lead with the Humber heavy armoured car Crusader driven by Sergeant Wilf Mould out in front. There had been no opposition so far that day but they were still advancing with caution under Red expecting the enemy to make themselves known at any time. There had been no hints or warnings from the locals but bitter experience in the past had taught them to rely on their own instincts and add to that any available local knowledge.

By 13.30 hrs he had entered the outskirts of Loenen driving along Eerbeeksweg when he spotted a tree felled across the road. He knew what this meant. The crew were now on high alert and radioed back about their find. On the left was a provisions store on the right ahead was the ruins of a burnt-out building. It was this building that attracted their attention, Wilf slowed, nerves jangling; they were now less than 50 metres away from the derelict building if anything was going to happen it was going to happen soon. Then they saw it, a movement in the ruins, the telltale tail flare of the rocket-propelled Panzerfäust. The German's aim was good enough to hit the car. Fortunately it did not penetrate the armour. The gunner Trooper Thomas had got a shot off in the direction of the house but before he could reload and re-sight, the car started to brew. Now was the time to use in earnest the practised scramble-out routine. From the driver's position the lower escape door was behind him on the left hand side. As he wriggled out of his seat Lance Corporal Macey and Trooper Thomas had made their escape through the top hatches just above their heads. Bent double Wilf yanked on the door release handle and with a heave-ho the door swung open. He rolled out onto the roadway. As he recovered he stood up to make a dash for the safety of the store, however, his pistol slipped from its holster. As Wilf thought that it could come in pretty handy sooner rather than later he bent back down again to recover it. As he did, he heard the crack of a bullet as it parted the air that had just been vacated by his head. He was now the centre of attention and with his car brewing he knew that he had limited time to make his escape. Fortunately the road was straight at this point and that enabled the following car to bring down supporting fire whilst he ran back to the cover of the nearby shops. The three crew members were all recovered without injury. From a secure distance the presence of determined opposition was reported back to squadron HQ with a request for assistance. Judge was to take no chances since he had no idea of the strength of the opposing force and how were they deployed? He set out his plan and later that day "C" Squadron returned in strength quelling the opposition and liberating the town. That night thirty prisoners of war accompanied "C" Squadron back to their harbour in Arnhem where they were forwarded to their own resting camp to have no further action in the war.

The on the 17th April "C" Squadron continued to push out westwards in the direction of Lunteren and patrol towards the Grebbe Line. The Grebbe line established in 1745 was a Dutch defensive line mostly a water defence achieved by inundation stretching from Ijsselmeer in the north via Amersfoort and Rhenen to the River Waal in the south finishing near a town familiar to the 49th; Druten. As 2 and 7 Troops moved towards De Klomp they came up against strong defensive opposition. This was a result of General Model's idea to utilise some of the Grebbe Line called the Pantherstellung. The Germans wanted to protect the Ijsselmeer region of Holland as they did not want to lose their ability to fire the V-2 rocket at London so therefore the Grebbe line was adapted to prevent the Allies from advancing in that direction. Five Kilometres to the northwest of De Klomp was a town called Renswoude where there was one of those all important bridges. A Large party lead by Lieutenant Giles complete with self-propelled guns under command made a wide circuitous route around the right flank and reached the bridge. After a brief struggle the bridge was seized and then to their dismay they were recalled by the division and with great difficulty as it was then dark they withdrew leaving the Germans to occupy the bridge once more. The reason only became clear later as an armistice was agreed to permit a food convoy to use that bridge to reach the starving Dutch.

The following day they were urgently called to concentrate at Apeldoorn for what was to be operation Elite. With tanks self-propelled guns, sappers and infantry under command they were ordered to make a lightning sweep due north towards the Zuyder Zee. As it turned out it was a bit of an anticlimax as there was no opposition and only a few stragglers were picked up, the majority had escaped across the Zee to Amsterdam.

Major Judge had managed during the campaign so far to find himself in difficult situations which happily were resolved in his favour. One afternoon in the vicinity of Elburg a marauding Spitfire found a moving target. Positioning the vehicle in the rings of his gun sight the pilot moved his thumb and pressed the firing button on his control column. He watched the tracers mark the path of his cannon fire as they curved towards the vehicle. He watched the ground erupt as they tracked towards the vehicle. He watched the strike on the vehicle, saw the vehicle swerve as the driver realised he was under attack and with another bogie struck off the list the Spitfire without a backward glance rose into the sky looking for another target. His report when he returned to base would have been wrong since he had successfully knocked out the Humber light armoured car commanded by Major Harry Judge. Although the car was lost only the wireless operator Corporal S. Nixon was wounded and Judge lost his valise and bedding.

With operation Elite completed the Squadron returned to patrolling the Grebbe Line near Renswoude where once again the Squadron Leader's car attracted more attention. With fate still on his side Judge escaped unhurt although both his crew Lance Corporal Nash and Sergeant Sharpe were wounded, This was the second time that Sergeant Sharpe had been wounded and this time he also picked up the honour of becoming the last casualty incurred by "C" Squadron.

They never had the opportunity to retake the bridge and the earlier battle remained their final engagement of the war as on the 25th April they received orders that all offensive operations were to cease with the formal surrender of the Germans in Holland taking place on 4th May 1945.

On the 7th of May the Squadron led the advance into West Holland with "A" Squadron entering Utrecht, "B" Squadron Hilversham and Amsterdam whilst "C" Squadron took the local German surrender in Baarn and Amersfoort. The Germans accepted and fulfilled their obligations of the local surrender and no opposition was encountered. The biggest impediment to movement was given by the civilians and it was with the greatest difficulty that the vehicles were able to force their way through the wildly enthusiastic crowds. Once the German surrender and handover had taken place followed by a bit of organisation the vulnerable points were handed over to the Dutch resistance.

The squadron then became involved in the dumping of ammunition and mines. Particular attention had to be given to ensure that the surrender was proceeding according to the agreed terms especially with regard to the HQ and associated companies of the German 88 Corps. They also escorted prisoners which included 60 Officers, 700 other ranks and 301 motor transports.

The following month on the 4th of June they took part in their final operation. After almost a year to the day from when they had first set foot in France they were in Germany to help complete the occupation of Germany. With Germany defeated Operation Overlord was completed and replaced by the final operation called Eclipse. That involved them in a move from Holland via Neunkirchen north of Osnabruck to Hüsten, Arnsberg in Westphalia, Germany where they carried out the final phase of occupation and completed their role in the liberation of Europe from Nazi domination.

One of the last acts in 1945 by the 49th Recce was to apply for and get granted official sanction to incorporate the special regimental distinction of superimposing a small white rose of York onto its Corps badge.

Chapter 18   The Recovery

Jimmie's reassessment on 1st March cheered him as it showed that there had been a progression in his recovery and as anticipated he was changed from a Category D to Category C. This was psychologically good for him since it meant that he was no longer of zero use to the army, at least he could do something on the Home Front should it be needed.

Nancy visited Jimmie again in March, the journey falling into the previous pattern except for this time she had to change trains at Didcot for the local train to Oxford. The change of trains did not phase her, she just hoped that Jimmie would realise and wasn't left fretful at Oxford station thinking that something had happened to her. Light of foot she came over the station bridge and out towards the road. Her eyes were scanning the crowd for the identifying white bonnet. It was not to be seen. Had he thought that she was not coming and returned to the hospital all down at heart? No matter she knew the bus to catch it was the number 2 bus to Kidlington and get off at the St Margaret's Road stop, so she would not let him down instead surprise him at St Hughes. It was the eyes and that tash she recognised in the waiting crowd as she came through the station exit. He had waited.

She enjoyed the walk through the town hanging on his arm, looking in shop windows and just chatting away about how Peter had grown and that Bert was okay wherever he was in India or was it Burma. She couldn't tell from his letters home but guessed from the newsreel reports of the fighting in the east. Jimmie explained that the loss of the white bonnet meant that his wound was well and truly on the mend. Nancy noticed that his hair was almost back to its swept-back look and the deep wave just over his right forehead was returning. Her Jimmie was returning to his former self. She expressed some anxiety over the improvement to Category C for fear that she might lose him again to the battlefield and perhaps he wouldn't be so lucky the next time. He assured her that he would not be called upon for front line work again and would most probably be restricted to the home front and that was as safe as she was so there was no need for her to worry. He confided in her that there had been indications that he would be released from hospital soon and could continue convalescence at home. Nancy was overjoyed and asked when that was likely to happen. If it does he told her it would be at the next review on the 1st of April.

All too soon the hands on the clock had chased each other round to their parting time. Once again they found themselves facing each other on the station, Nancy leaning from the train window. The parting words were different, this time it was a farewell by Jimmie saying that next time he would see her in Belvedere. Then the whistle, flag waving and the little jig by the coaches brought about their parting.

The days of March seemed to be endless and then on 27th March, a few days earlier than expected he was called to see the MO. The MO read his notes and after some questions and a cursory examination of his physical wounds told him he had improved but was not as yet fully recovered. After five months at St Hughes twice the average length of stay he was going to be released not back to the services but to remain on sick leave with the final part of his recovery to be spent at home. He could swap the Hospital Blues and the white mop bonnet for his uniform and peaked cap. He could leave immediately and was given instructions to report in a month's time to his local hospital in Woolwich.

By the time the paperwork was completed the rest of the week had evaporated. On Saturday morning 31st March he had the release order and a travel warrant to Belvedere in his pocket. He walked the corridors and wards of St Hugh's shaking many hands whilst saying his thanks to the surgeons and nurses and his best wishes to his fellow blue-uniformed white bonneted patients. He opened the front door for the last time and stepped out into St Margret's Road and walked to the bus stop in the warm springtime sunshine that Oxford was bathed in that weekend.

It was strange to feel rather than see the joggle of the carriages as the couplings took up the strain. To watch the station slip past seeing the waving arms of those left behind. Then onwards, shortly to cross the Thames or as it is known locally the Isis, whose waters in 130 miles would flow past Belvedere as it surged its way out into the estuary before being absorbed by the sea. In time the countryside gave way to houses and those gave way to the devastation of the suburbia around London and then opened out towards the countryside again although the stain of bomb damage was still in evidence as he drew closer to his destination. Had his latest letter to Nancy arrived? Would she be there to meet him? As Abbey Wood was left behind he would soon know the answers. Either way it wouldn't be long now before he would be able to see and hold her again for longer than those brief times in Oxford and there was Peter as well who he was longing to get to know.

The answer to his questions came as the train entered Belvedere Station for he saw her there waiting for him pram in hand with Peter sitting up not knowing the importance of the next few minutes. He went to wave but the sight of her was lost behind the station buildings. The private tri-union was just a prelude to the hugs and handshakes that he was to receive accompanied by cups of tea. He was home, at least for a month, maybe more who knew and he was going to take full advantage of it until he was signed off and had to return to duty.

The first few weeks of home leave was used not only to enjoy time with Nancy and Peter but also to improve his stamina after being inactive for so long. They enjoyed the walks in Franks Park, picnics in the countryside and the meanders along the river where they might just wonder if this was some of the water that had passed around Oxford whilst he was there. He also started to take up woodworking again and made a Peter sized armchair which Nancy and he covered. Peter proudly placed this in their living room and would sit there with the adults smoking his pretend wooden pipe that his dad had also made for him.

Jimmie reported to the hospital at Woolwich on 27th April and was still categorised as "C" much the same as he was the previous month at Oxford. He was to remain on home leave for at least another three weeks.

The blitz was now a thing of the past and the last V2 fell on the East End on 27th March. The war seemed far away. He would read the newspapers, listen to the news on the wireless trying to interpret the war news to find out how the boys in his "C" Squadron were doing. There was news of rapid advances especially in Holland and he knew that the Recce would be there, keeping to their motto – "Only the enemy in front" leading the way in this final surge to victory. It was just a case of how much longer the great German Military regime could survive. It wasn't to be much longer.

At a quarter to three in the morning of the 7th May Germany unconditionally surrendered. Jimmie at home in Belvedere with Peter, Nancy and her parents gathered in their upstairs living room around the wireless. They listened to Churchill's radio broadcast giving the news for which everybody was waiting. A quietness fell in the room as the announcement was made:-

> *"The Prime Minister the right honourable*
> *Winston Churchill"*

"Yesterday morning at 2.41 am at General Eisenhower's Head Quarters General Jodel the representative of the German High Command and of Grand Admiral Donitz the designated head of the German State signed the act of unconditional surrender of all German Land Sea and Air Forces in Europe to the Allied Expeditionary Force ..... "

The war in Europe was over. The great celebrations of VE day started. At Lower Road it was not all rejoicing as their son, Nancy's brother Bert was still fighting with the 'forgotten army' in Burma. Their worries and concerns whilst alleviated as far as Jimmie was concerned now fully concentrated on the war against Japan and the plight of Bert.

Through the post came another buff envelope and hearts raced again at the dreadful thought that this was bad news of Bert. The envelope was addressed to Jimmie so whilst there was relief about Bert it brought news that Jimmie's sojourn in Kent was over. He had been posted to 161st Recce Regiment in Newcastle with effect from 18th May.

Although the war in Europe was over it still continued against Japan so the latest news on the wireless was listened to on a regular basis. Almost one of the last broadcasts that they listened to as a family group heard the news on 19th May. Karl Lehmann who was working for the BBC Monitoring Service reported that German radio had announced earlier the death of Adolf Hitler. This led to Jimmie's leg being pulled that Hitler had heard of Jimmie's reporting on the 18th and couldn't stand the thought of Jimmie's return.

His sick leave ran out on 23rd May so on the 24th he reported for duty in Newcastle at the 161st Recce HQ. The 161st Recce Regiment was one of the feeder units to where the injured reported once they had recovered from their injury and were ready for service again. Whilst it was possible to request to be sent back to your original unit this was denied to Jimmie as he remained Category "C" and consequently could not go into front line operations. Although the war in Europe was over there was still the thorny matter of Japan and the services out there could do with replacements and so the work of the 161st Recce continued.

In less than two months after VE Day the Labour party under the leadership of Clement Attlee fought the first general election since 1935. Their manifesto slogan of "Let Us Face the Future", created a swing of 9.7% sufficient to give them a comfortable majority. Jimmie was furious with the result. He could not understand why a man who had guided the country through a world war should be so savagely thrown on the political scrap heap.

Medically as well as militarily Jimmie remained under the eye of the Military. On 27th July this meant another report to the MO, this time at Newcastle. By now he was used to the procedure and whilst he felt better he was still only graded as Category "C". However with the war over and a wife and child as his new responsibilities he was more readily inclined to accept that his days as a fighting soldier were over.

Although Jimmie was on the home front, albeit wounded, Nancy's brother Bert, who had introduced her to Jimmie, was still at war in the Far East against Japan, but the good news was soon to follow in August. With Victory in Europe less than three months old the allies were contemplating the use of a new tactical weapon that they had developed. The attritional costs to the allies of continuing the fight against an enemy who believed it better to die fighting than it was to talk peace was high. They had a possible solution and Enola Gay a United States Army Air Forces Boeing B-29 Superfortress bomber, named after the mother of the pilot, Colonel Paul Tibbets became on the 6th August 1945 the instrument to carry and drop on Hiroshima the first atomic bomb. Three days later on the 9th of August another United States Army, Air Forces B-29 bomber called Bockscar dropped a Fat Man nuclear weapon over the Japanese city of Nagasaki making it the second – and hopefully last – nuclear attack in history. It wreaked utter devastation with 150,000 casualties in those two cities. In the face of such devastation the Japanese Emperor, Hirohito, acknowledged defeat and brought about the surrender of the Japanese forces.

This brought to an end Bert's war and this time a more meaningful celebration in Lower Road.

With the world in a transient peace there came the problems associated with the end of aggression. The armed forces and prisoners of war had to be brought home. For many demobilisation would take years, with some service personnel returning to families and homes they hadn't seen for more than five years. It was to help in this that Jimmie was given a command. For the uninitiated it might not appear a big task, just a case of sticking the figurative stamp on their forehead and sending them home. But it wasn't. Few people realised what a huge effort and the amount of work that would be involved to repatriate prisoners of war. In Germany alone there were over 1,000 Kriegsgefangenenlager with a total of 170,000 POWs and in Japan another 56,000 were held but because Japan did not fully comply with the Geneva Convention these numbers were inaccurate and the number of POW camps was unknown until after the war. Fortunately Jimmie only had to manage the problem on the home front. It was someone else's problem to marshal them from the multitude of camps and get them to his receiving depot at Newcastle.

Before any ex-POWs arrived a system had to be devised so that the information required was gathered in the most efficient and practical way. Each returning soldier that arrived at Newcastle had to be medically examined, clothed, paid his back dues and sent on a 28 day leave. A practice routine was worked through to enable the various groups of doctors, dentists, ophthalmologist, pay clerks and stores personnel to know what was required of them and for which part of the twenty forms that had to be accurately completed for each man they were responsible. It was also explained to them how they fitted into the overall scheme so they could act as one large team.

As well as collating the information required they had to consider the effect of exaggerated and unnecessary delays in the process. After being held in captivity for a long time the ex-POW's would be buoyed up with the expectancy of seeing their loved ones again and any delays would be frustrating and seem an eternity. They would be expecting troops in by the train or boatload and had decided to break them down into manageable groups of thirty which could be accommodated in the standard Nissen hut barracks. Each hut provided with its own NCOs and orderlies. One hut at a time could then be processed; in their practice run they looked for any bottlenecks which would be alleviated by increasing the local capacity to enable the desired smooth and rapid flow.

Notification of the first train was received, it was due to arrive mid-afternoon at Newcastle Central, bringing 187 repatriated prisoners of war from various camps in Germany. A fleet of transport trucks was despatched to meet them. Jimmie as Commanding Officer would be accompanied by a Quarter Master to give his own welcome to the returning troops. Members of the Depot staff would also go to the station. As the lorries filled they left for the main camp and debussed on the main parade ground where they were separated into groups of thirty, introduced to their hut NCO's and then marched off to their hut, their baggage, what little they had, followed on behind. A welcoming brew and biscuits were made available in each hut and then it was down to business.

One hut at a time went through the process and the twenty forms got completed. It was not a case of having to march between examinations since the rooms were organised sequentially, starting with the physical medical exam followed by the dentist, then optician, then it was to the stores for a new kit which could include inter alia medal ribbons, rank badges, service chevrons and cap badges. Last but not least a visit to the ablutions block for the three S's. This was followed by a special welcoming meal when the local band provided musical entertainment in the evening.

The following day they were issued with their back pay, a 28 day leave pass and a travel warrant home.

At the time whilst depression and shell shock were known common mental disorders suffered by soldiers, post-traumatic stress disorder (aka PTSD) was still waiting to be appreciated. Jimmie and his team had been prepared for some of the post prison camp problems they might have to handle. Most of the returnees were buoyed up by the fact that they were back in England and would soon be seeing their loved ones again be they parents, wives, children or that special someone that they had met last time on leave. Beneath that thin veneer of energy would be some very tired and exhausted bodies thus it was essential to ensure they were processed quickly and as soon as possible.

It didn't take long before the stories started to do the rounds. There was the episode of one returnee who expressed his joy that after having been restricted to a compound surrounded by barbed wire for many months how good it felt when he got home to be able to open any door and go through it without having somebody with a rifle say he couldn't. Then there was the contrapositive of the soldier when first arriving home woke on the first morning back, opened the front door and walked up to the front garden gate but couldn't walk through it and returned indoors.

There was also the sad tales of the soldiers who returned to their parent's home or to their wife to find that they had been casualties of bombing raids and the only welcome home was by a razed building.

The cruelty of war and the homecoming continued for the soldiers whose girlfriends had found another whilst they were away. But this was mild compared to those that found their wives with a child in tow. She would try and convince her husband that he was older than the date of his last 48-hour pass. There were other times when the woman was not there, she had disappeared off with another, sometimes putting several thousands of miles of water between them.

In December he had been commanding the repatriation section for six months and thought that it would be a good time to put in a formal request for his previous rank of Captain, that he had to relinquish in Porthcawl in 1942, to be reinstated. This was considered by the Senior Executive Officer and on the 19th of December in time for Christmas he once again became Captain J.E. Knox a title that he was to keep this time around.

When the POW's from the Far East arrived it was a heart wrenching sight. To see these proud men as skin and bone deprived of the basic nourishments whilst in captivity. Some had been the subject of man's inhumanity to man by a nation that believes that it was better to die in battle and that a prisoner was the lowest of the low. There were the few after having survived through all the deprivations possible return home to find that they then have to suffer from woman's disloyalty to man.

Jimmie was shattered at the way some wives had acted whilst their husbands were prisoners and it was on those occasions that the help of the local Padre or Rabbi was sought and perhaps the good auspices of the Red Cross, the Order of St John or the Legion would be invoked and where they could all parties helped the returning soldier to recuperate from not only his traumas of war but also those on his return.

The repatriation work continued through the early part of 1946, when March arrived the repatriation numbers had dwindled and after helping so many others it became Jimmie's turn to be considered for demob. He had to attend Corsham for what turned out to be his last medical. The result remained basically unchanged as a Category "C" although his grading within that category had improved. On 8th March 1946 he was struck off the unit strength and given leave until 3rd May whereupon on the 4th May he ceased to be employed by His Majesty and like his father before him at the end of the First World War, he was discharged with a disability pension.

A new life lay ahead of him with all its challenges, its ups and downs as he said au revoir to the services and returned to the civilian life he had left in September 1939.

The war had passed through the town of Loenen and moved on sweeping its way across the rest of northern Holland. Once again the town's people were free and slowly food began to appear and they enjoyed this first taste of freedom. The tree had been removed, the burnt out armoured car, the first into the town on that day of liberation still remained where it had been hit. The local children were using it as a playground, re-enacting its last battle or other imaginary ones as they played at winning the war. Eventually during the inevitable clearing up of the detritus of war a heavy towing vehicle arrived one day in the town. The armoured car that had been called Crusader, the focal point of discussions and visits especially by the school children was hitched up and taken away. It was towed north further along Eerbeeksweg than it had previously reached and then along Groenendaalseweg until they had left the town behind. After a kilometre there was a track off to the right, they towed Mould's armoured car sufficiently that it was out of sight and dumped it in the trees behind an attractive thatched house called Klein Iwalt (Little Iwalt) and then the lorry left.

All of a sudden it was the 7th of May, just a few weeks after Loenen's liberation the whole of Holland was free from the Nazi scourge and celebrations were in order. The following day another excuse to continue the celebrations as Germany capitulated and the death of Hitler was announced. Slowly Europe returned to some form of non-war normality and some had time to consider what they had lived through and the impact of that day in April when the town was liberated. Would someone want a souvenir?

It was Mr Pulle and his son Frederik that had the idea of keeping some memento of the war and their ultimate liberation and they had an inspiration. On Sunday 12th August after lunch father and son went for a walk along the track behind Klein Iwalt and found that Sergeant Mould's car was still there. It was a bit worse for standing four months in the woods but it was still there. They pulled away some of the growth that was slowly enveloping it to uncover the main turret and gun. They made a good examination of the gun and its fixings because it was the gun they had decided that they wanted as a souvenir. Between them they decided that it could be removed and they made a list of the tools that were required. They then returned home excited that their idea could be accomplished. The following day they returned with the tools they thought were necessary. They worked for most of the day and the following day gradually stripping away parts of the interior and chipped away the thick paint over the bolt heads. After a lot of hard work, one by one the bolts were removed until the gun was free. They decided to leave it until Wednesday to finally remove the gun and bring it back.

The weather on Wednesday remained fair. Reinier and Frederik set off from their home of De Looijenboom situated on the opposite side of Groenendaalseweg to the gun. They walked they hoped for the last time, the 400 metres to the car. That day they took a stout wheelbarrow and some strong rope together with their tools. They had every intention of bringing the gun back that day. There was a lot of heaving and pulling before eventually, the gun tumbled from its position on the turret and fell to the ground. After a breather the two managed to get the breech positioned in the wheelbarrow with the barrel of the gun pointing forward. They decided that there was no point in tying the gun to the wheelbarrow as it would only hinder any recovery should the thing tip over. They tied the rope to the front of the wheelbarrow and with Reinier as the dray and Frederik as the steady at the back they set off for De Looijenboom. So it was that on the same day that the world was relieved of the terror of Japan so the armoured car was relieved of its gun something the world's press missed but not the local press.

Given that this was mostly an exercise in movement through the woods with only a brief run along the road Mr Pulle was surprised when the police paid him a visit, fearing the worst when they asked to see the gun. The police were not interested in how the gun was acquired but more concerned about the rumour that there was a live round in the breech. On finding the rumour false they departed leaving the gun to be kept by Mr Pulle and his family as a private trophy and memorial to the men that had liberated their village.

Pulle built a cairn made from cobblestones in his back garden and onto the top he proudly mounted the gun. The direction in which the gun pointed was not only towards the town of Loenen but also in the direction of Berlin. For the next 33 years the gun remained in the garden as a souvenir and perhaps a warning to any second coming of Hitler.

The Gun on its Way to De Looijenboom

A Souvenir at Home

PART THREE

After the War

Chapter 19   *A Civilian at Home*

England had changed during the period of the war. Gone were its old Imperialistic notions. Instead a new more egalitarian attitude prevailed with new industries, born in the war, taking over from the old traditional ones. For Jimmie it was going to take on another dimension for when he returned home at the start of his release leave Nancy had some exciting news for him. She was so excited she just couldn't wait until the following month to make it a birthday surprise she had to tell him immediately now that she knew – she was late. With this news in mind they decided that it would be a good time to go away together to have that honeymoon made impossible by the war. Since they had enjoyed Ireland so much they decided to take up the offer made to them when they left Ireland. They wrote to the owners of the farm in Caledon asking if they could take up that offer and come and stay with them for a short holiday. Ireland had no hesitation an enthusiastic "yes" came back in the post.

They, that's Jimmie, Nancy and Peter were waved off from Belvedere Station by Bert and his new wife Mary. Who coincidentally had the maiden name of Knox. It was an electric train that took them into London and then a steam train that carried them north to Carlisle and on to the Ferry. The weather for the crossing was wet and windy which gave a typically rough crossing. Fortunately Jimmie was able to acquire a cabin where Nancy could try and overcome the sickness, sea or morning was unknown.

By the time they had arrived in Caledon the sun had won the battle of the skies and bathed the lush greens of the countryside in warm sunlight. After the initial welcoming hugs and handshakes and a genuine interest in Peter they were all delighted at Nancy's news. They were shown to their old room; although it had been redecorated in the intervening years it smelt like they remembered. Life settled down to be as comfortable as old slippers. The routine of the farm hadn't changed and after a bit of practice Nancy found that she had not forgotten her earlier learnt skills of milking. Jimmie unencumbered by the duties of his rank had more time to spend with Peter. He would take Peter every morning egg hunting in the hayloft and then they would play at jumping from the top of the stacked bales to land on the broken straw bales on the ground. Afterwards they would walk the country lanes taking Peter to see the blue and red parrot that lived in a cage just by the junction at the top of the hill. Take car rides into the larger towns of Armagh and Newry for what would now be called retail therapy. All too soon time had passed by and they had to say farewell again to their Irish friends. They were to leave and this time whilst the open invitation to visit was made circumstances were such that it was never taken up and after a few years, communication between them drifted into nothingness.

As well as getting used to civilian working again he also had to find a home for his wartime bride, son and one on the way. Until now Nancy together with his son had lived with her parents in Belvedere, a mile or so across the Thames from the Ford Motor works at Dagenham, in what must have been bomb alley. With a second child on the way and with Bert who had married in 1941 now wishing to bring his wife, who was also pregnant with her first child, down from Selby to Belvedere it would become very crowded at 239 Lower Road. Jimmie wanted to move back to Wimbledon, where his family lived. He placed himself on the Council waiting list for a property and waited. In just over a month the Council offered him a flat in Melbury Gardens in the area of Cottenham Park just half a kilometre from where he was born and a kilometre from where his mother lived. It was also an easy walk to Raynes Park Station that he had used previously to get him to work. The option of number 77 was taken and the three of them moved in the late summer. By this time

Nancy was heavily pregnant and with Jimmie working hard they decided that the best place for Nancy to have her baby was back in Belvedere with her mother caring for her. On the 8th of November their second child was born in the same hospital in Erith as Peter. The return to Raynes Park happened after the Christening service in the local church of Saint Fidelis in West Street Erith when Graham Anthony became a member of the Roman Catholic Church, Jimmie again keeping to his promise made when he married.

Christmas of 1946 was to be their first Christmas as a family of four and they were going to rejoice in it together at 77 Melbury Gardens. Money was tight and fortunately the demands were not that great. Graham was happy watching the candles flicker on a small Christmas tree or the fire in the grate. Peter was happy with a couple of toys they bought, added to which there were presents from the grandparents and a big bag of sweets from Ireland. Any spare cash went on furnishing the flat as they had started with nothing. The days of white goods wish lists and easy credit on plastic were yet to come so it was essentials first together with make and mend. The weather had been kind to them with temperatures reaching into the mid-double figures. Then on the 23rd of January it all changed. Six weeks of snow started with easterly winds bringing a succession of snowstorms across the UK making it the snowiest winter since the mid-nineteenth century. The temperatures were low and with no thaw between the storms the depth of snow increased. Nationwide the storms caused severe hardships in economic terms and living conditions as the country tried to recover from the war. There were massive disruptions of energy supply for homes, offices and factories. For Jimmie there was a continuous search for wood and coal for the open fires. At times these were difficult to find and questionable methods had to be employed to ensure that the fires would keep burning.

When the thaw came in late March there were problems of burst pipes and for number 77 leaks in the roof that required a procession of pots pans and buckets to catch the water as it dripped from the ceilings. After the problems of the flat during that severe winter, they put in a request to the Council for another. In the summer they had the opportunity to move to number 92 Cambridge Road. Unfortunately this flat had its problems and after their continuous badgering of the Council they were given a large first floor two bedroomed apartment a few doors away at number 88. This was to become their home for the next six years.

With only a handful of years having passed since the end of the war conflict was again raising its head this time in Korea. For Jimmie though the 1950s opened with the birth of their third child. This time there was no return to have the baby at Belvedere, Nancy's mother came to stay to help her and to look after the two boys. Lynda Jean was born on 31st January at St Teresa's nursing home, run by Nuns, it was situated on a road called The Downs just off Wimbledon Common. The arrival of a girl obviously completed a hidden wish and their family was completed with the daughter.

During the Housing boom of the middle 1930s as a young man he had seen the development of the fields and orchards in which he had played as a boy. The road leading directly from the south side of Raynes Park station was called Grand Drive and the houses built along it were large houses and as the road name implies he thought that they were grand as well. With his growing family number 88 with just two bedrooms was becoming cramped and problematic. Even with the increased family burden they had been saving over the years and now decided that they should try and enter into the property market. They searched through the sprawling new developments in Motspur and Worcester Park before his heart brought him to decide on a large two reception, three bedroomed house in Grand Drive. On 8th October 1953 he bought and moved into number 162 one of the houses that when he was young to own was only a pipe dream. Now it was a dream come true, large enough for the boys to have their own bedroom and Lynda hers. Over time he once again used his carpentry ability and built his own fitted kitchen. He then bought his first car and that needed a home so he added bricklaying and roofing to his skills by building an attached garage. Number 162, he subsequently called "Petgralyn", an anagram of his three children's names, was where he remained. He watched his children grow, marry, leave home and return with their children in the space of the next forty-five years.

In the early years of their family, money was something that was never plentiful but with care and hard work he was managing to improve his standard of living. The new neighbours introduced him to children's private education. Peter had already slipped through the net and had just started his secondary education. Graham although at primary school was at an age where he could benefit. Jimmie had a word with Head Mistress, Mrs Strickland, of the local school called St David's to which the other neighbours sent their children. She was prepared to let him enrol Graham whom he did and managed to eke out his earnings so to do.

The private education proved beneficial for Graham as it enabled him to pass the 11+ to get into the school of his choice. 1957 saw Graham walk down the same road in Wimbledon as Jimmie had 29 years earlier and enter the gates of the old Wimbledon Central School which was now a Grammar School and had returned to its original name of Pelham. Lynda went on to be educated at St David's but alas the hard earned money did not allow her to reap any educational advantage.

They were now on the rising tide of the period known as the swinging sixties when the teenagers were joining the

CND, with "Ban the bomb" marches, there was flower power with a liberal spread of free love. Their parents' generation were also enjoying this period. Mrs Strickland held her Christmas parties with her versions of children's games for the parents all liberally helped along the way with a generous helping of alcohol. There were anecdotes about the fun of the game "Sardines", which for those who have not had the experience of playing is loosely based on the game of hide and seek except when you find the nominated person instead of revealing their hiding place you join them. The school was in a large house and with everywhere available to hide led to great fun especially when multiple adults were trying to hide themselves in a space in which not as many children would fit.

When one of your neighbours are from north of the border where Christmas celebrations had been banned for over 400 years by the straight-laced Kirk as being Popish, party time is a week later. Although the virtual ban on Christmas in Scotland had ended in the 1950s the party still remains a week later at Hogmanay, the Scottish word for the last day of the year. With Willie and Wendy Hillhouse the tradition of farewell to the old and welcome to the New Year was cause for the biggest party of the year. Immediately after midnight with Nancy at their piano they would link cross armed and sing Auld Lang Syne after which they would have the tradition of "First Footing" where one dark haired gentleman was sent outside to return with the traditional lump of coal. Then there was whiskey galore until the party broke up. On at least one occasion Nancy led the departing partygoers in a Conga down the white line in the middle of Grand Drive with neighbours leaving as they passed their homes, some even overshot.

St David's school was expanding and needed extra indoor space. Here again Jimmie's carpentry skills helped out and he together with other parents gave up their weekends and built the required hall in part of the school's playground.

The world kept on turning and as night follows day the children grew. Peter went on to further education at Ewell Technical College in Jimmie's eyes only fair that he supported him at this end of his education as he hadn't been able to in the beginning. The earth found itself for a short period of time with a man-made moon called Sputnik heralding the imminent arrival of the exploration if not the exploitation of worlds beyond our own. For Jimmie is was to be the end of an era one he had started nearly a quarter of a century ago when he entered the Drill hall in Wimbledon and signed up to serve King and Country. On the first of July 1959 he relinquished his Commission keeping the title of Captain, which incidentally he never used. The old drill hall survived a few more years before Lloyds bank knocked it down in order to build their new offices and the council changed the parade ground into a multi-story car park, oh how things have changed.

Peter was the first to leave home, even if it was initially only on a part-time basis. He went to Brighton to attend one of the latest generations of top technical colleges or CATs as they were called. (CAT being an anagram for College of Advanced Technology now it has become Brighton University) It was during this period that Peter got his first car a 1936 blue Austin Seven Ruby registration DPG 223. It was supped-up with straight-through exhaust, a big downdraft Zenith carburettor and in the end not that reliable. There was one occasion when Peter was still a learner that he and his colleagues had taken the car one Bank Holiday Monday to the White Lion pub in Cobham only to find that it wouldn't start again when the drinking had stopped. The AA could not turn out until the following day so Peter went the next day to the pub and waited for the AA to get it started. Once it was running Jimmie made his way there by train to Cobham and sat as the qualified driver as Peter drove home. Keen to show off its speed the homeward journey began. They were still two and a half miles and a hill away from home when there was a loud bang from the engine and then it all went quiet. It took a long time for the two of them to push the car home which they eventually did, arriving well after midnight. Having re-visited the route over which we had pushed the car I just don't know how we managed it. We must have been very fit and strong.

The sixties came to an end with mixtures of highs and lows. The first high was that his membership of the Freemasons after fourteen years as a member had reached its climax as he became the Master of his Lodge Con Amore. He subsequently became Lodge Secretary and in 1980 was awarded Senior London Grand Rank, which he held until he died. Then in 1968 Peter married his fiancé Pat and he then truly became the first of the family to permanently leave the nest. Then there was the low. It wasn't that it came as a surprise for his mother had been ill for some time but when the bad news came on the 6th of June 1969 it was still a shock.

His family life continued in the next decade to be just as busy. His daughter Lynda got married in December 1970. Early the next year he became a double grandfather. Firstly he was presented with a granddaughter Deborah by his daughter and then shortly afterwards with a grandson Christopher, by Pat. October 1973 saw the arrival of his third grandchild Paul to his daughter. Two years later Pat made him a grandfather for the fourth time with the arrival of her second son Simon. Christmases were getting expensive! It was to be almost another ten years before his daughter provided his fifth and final grandchild Barry.

Meanwhile in parallel with his domesticity his life in the world of commerce had its ups and downs and changes.

Relaxing at Home

Chapter 20   A Civilian at Work

Electricity was one of the new industries; this was to prove to be an asset to Jimmie who now had to pick up the pieces of his career in journalism. He had returned to work at the Electrical Times and found at first that the change from commanding a large number of men working under a strict routine to working with only a few people in an office was difficult.

By the 50's he had worked his way up at the ET to become responsible for production. Then he was to find that not everything goes smoothly. Having got his little production unit working well the unions called a printers strike. This would cause chaos in his department and threaten the very existence of the journal. It was his responsibility to get the ET published there was no passing it off to anybody else. He had an appreciation of the power of the unions especially the print union. He was fully aware that if he simply tried to use a small provincial printer the unions would make it difficult for the printer to work. He even considered getting it printed on the continent but was advised that the continental unions would support their British brothers. His wartime experience told him there was always some way of achieving the impossible. He drew from that experience as he rose to the challenge of getting the issues published. Having harboured in several Convents and Nunneries during the war Jimmie knew that they were a law unto themselves and would be impervious to the pleas of the unions. His solution was simple; he would find a Nunnery with a printing press on the near continent, supply them with the art blocks and get them to print the ET. His searches proved successful, he found a French nunnery that published religious papers. His carpentry knowledge helped with the next part of the solution as he converted his offices into a carpenters shop and made the wooden crates to send the art blocks out to the "Sisters of the free press" as he called them. The classified section was tapped out on an old typewriter and the Headlines achieved with an amateur printing set and then married to the main issue as a loose flyer. The scheme worked, the ET survived and Jimmie's reputation was enhanced.

At heart he still had an impish nature where the pranks of his youth lurked just beneath the surface. For lunch he and a couple of chaps from the office frequented the pub nearby. They would have the requisite pint and perhaps a pie or a scotch egg or even a hardboiled egg from a dish on the counter. The eggs were left with their shells on presumably so that they could be offered again the next day. The usual technique for removing the shell was to crack it against the edge of your pint jug. To Jimmie this just invited trouble. It was a Friday that he decided that the trouble should occur and on that day he brought from home a raw egg. Lunchtime came, Jimmie and the raw egg left for the pub. He ordered his usual pint and opted to have a hardboiled egg with it. As he picked up his selected egg he left behind the one that he had brought from home. He then sat back, watched and waited. It wasn't long before another hungry drinker bought an egg not just an egg but the one Jimmie had left. From his vantage point Jimmie could see the next act in the story. The egg was carefully transported in the chaps right hand and his jug of beer in the other to a table next but one to where Jimmie sat. He looked across at Jimmie and smiled, Jimmie as courteous as ever smiled back although the smile had a hint of anticipation in it that the man didn't realise. He placed the jug and the egg on the table and sat down. First came a sup of ale then he picked up the egg and after a couple of practice taps on the jug went for it. He was expecting the shell to crack and the solid rubberiness of the egg to stop the motion. What happened instead was that the momentum of the hand carried the egg clean through the shell and with no solid inside to resist the pressure of his fingers the egg collapsed sending a split yoke shared between his drink, his fingers and the table via the outside of the jug. His automatic reaction was to draw back his hand and flick his wrist to clear the egg from his fingers which only transported the yoke to his jacket and face. This was more than Jimmie had expected but experience had taught him that to laugh now would be an end move. So with a deadpan face he lifted his own jug, finished the drink and left. The following week he heard all about the episode and what the barmaid was going to do with the culprit. Fortunately experience paid off as he was never uncovered as the instigator of the prank.

As he had found out in the services the usual prerequisite for an Officer of a bank account and Cert A had not stopped him from becoming an Officer. He succeeded then and he would succeed now. He had never been on any complex in-depth sales courses to help him in his climb to the position of Advertising Manager. His technique was to improvise on the spot and as he said, "sometimes there was a lot of improvisation in some very tight spots". No change from the Recce then.

The British magazine publishing industry in the mid-1950s in which Jimmie was involved was dominated by a handful of companies, principally the Associated Newspapers, Odhams, George Newnes Publishers, and the Hulton Press, which fought each other for market share in a highly competitive marketplace. In 1958 Cecil King, chairman of the newspaper group which included the *Daily Mirror* and the *Sunday Mirror* together with provincial chain West of England Newspapers, had an offer for Amalgamated Press accepted. In early 1959 he changed its name to Fleetway Publications then in 1961 went on to absorb Odhams Press, George Newnes and the Hulton Press. As a consequence, King controlled the publishing interests of the Mirror Group, along with almost one hundred consumer magazines, more than two hundred trade and technical periodicals as well as interests in book publishing. He managed to achieve all this without any significant change in management, save for the appointment of Mirror Group directors as chairmen. In 1963 all the companies were combined and called the

International Publishing Company or as it became known – IPC.

In all this mêlée of takeovers the ET passed through fundamentally unscathed so Jimmie's job was safe and by the 1960's he was running his own small but busy department at the ET from new offices in Dorset Buildings just off Fleet Street. However, no matter how safe he thought that his job was in 1966 after the ET came under the banner of the IPC group his department was closed down. Fortunately his services were still required and he moved with the paper to Bowling Green Lane.

A busy new decade was heralded in by decimalisation in February 1971, the introduction of VAT in 1973 and only having to work a 3 day week by 1974 by courtesy of Arthur Scargill and Ted Heath. At the end of the decade the Irish problem was brought to the fore with the death of Mountbatten whilst he was holidaying in his summer home of Classiebawn Castle in Mullaghmore. On 27th August 1979 this small seaside village in County Sligo was just 12 miles from the Northern Irish border was rocked by an IRA bomb placed on board Mountbatten's boat Shadow V with deadly results.

The colour of the government changed from Ted Heath's blue to the red of Harold Wilson and 'Honest' Jim Callaghan before reverting to blue again under the UK's first woman Prime Minister. There were technical leaps and bounds in the printing industry one of those introduced colour to the newspapers and then came computers. The change in tone of the Thatcher Government with new trade union legislation allowed employers to de-recognise unions. This enabled the big and bold print houses to challenge the Union's closed shop. Eddie Shah's Messenger Group was one of the companies that benefited enabling the group to use an alternative workforce and introduce new technology in newspaper production where journalists could input copy directly. Murdoch of News International saw how the technology could reduce labour in the print halls, cut costs and shorten production time dramatically. Murdoch built a new plant at Wapping using all the latest printing and publishing technology and once ready sacked all his old employees. Needless to say the unions were not happy and called a strike asking for support from other unions. Murdoch outwitted them, never lost a day's production and effectively got rid of the "hot metal" linotype newspaper production and that broke the union control in the printing industry.

For Jimmie too the decade was busy. After the ET became part of the IPC Electrical and Electronic Press, another office move was required, this time to Dorset House in Stamford Street still in Central London. New technology was in order and that brought changes to the look and style of the ET. The original black and white gave way to four colours on an A4 format and Jimmie's learning curve began again. In 1973 he increased the size of his department by successfully launching 2 journals and a yearbook. In recognition of this he was invited to join the Executive Board of the main technical group. Whilst this was indeed a feather in his cap he found the board room battles difficult to understand and consequently win all those he wanted. He was nearly a dinosaur in the boardroom outnumbered and outgunned by a new breed of university graduates who with a calculator and note pad argued in financial terms not in print and colour, loyalty base and image. He would come home frustrated with the New Blood in the ET and the group's management all of whom he found difficult to work with. "They don't understand journalism" he would say. Jimmie clung to his practical working knowledge, he still didn't have a Cert A but he had a bank account now and a wise head on his shoulders. Being ever watchful of the market in 1976 he saw an opportunity to launch another magazine called Middle East Electricity which became a success and made money. Then there was another change. The cost of the 4 colour A4 format was too much the university types said, we can make more money if we use the newspaper format of tabloid. Jimmie had no way to counter, quality and prestige amounted to not a jot and so the magazine went and a newspaper arrived.

In 1980 IPC Business Press moved to a new building, Quadrant House at Sutton in Surrey, just a few miles from his home in Grand Drive. When he looked back over his time in the industry he realised how much attitudes within it had changed since he first started selling display advertising space. Jimmie in his retirement interview said

> *"Twenty to thirty years ago there were more companies to sell to and business was done on a much more personal basis. Gone are companies like English Electric, BTH, Metropolitan Vickers and Hotpoint all gobbled up by GEC forming one conglomerate. In the original companies the man who booked advertising space had sole responsibility; his decision was very powerful. Now he hadn't got the freedom of action, he had to justify his decisions, and authorisation came from marketing departments. The industry was much more discriminating now about how it used advertising. People are far more discerning and need to know more about the journal; how its circulation figures broke down, for instance. Before they weren't so critical on response, now it's all about response."*

It wasn't long now before his sixty-fifth birthday and retirement. Before he said his goodbyes in April he still had a lot on his plate as he continued to expand the scope of his advertising department. In the meantime David Hall was appointed as his successor and he was going to find

Jimmie a hard act to follow. Jimmie had contributed much to the development of the paper since he started in the early 1930s and in that time had managed to get many of his clients to exceed their advertising budgets. He had a large number of friends in the industry and let them all know that he would be at the Electrex Exhibition at the NEC in February to say goodbye and thank you to as many that could come.

On 27th April 1982, his sixty-fifth birthday, after almost 50 years with the ET he cleared his desk as it was time to say goodbye to all his work colleagues. To do this he took advantage of the usual farewell party. Unfortunately his ultimate boss Keith Macdonald had been called away to America so it was perhaps for the better that his oldest friend at the journal, Ken Pounds the current publisher and editor replaced him as host. This worked well because having worked with Jimmie on the paper for a long time Ken was able to add those personal touches which only he knew about as he charted Jimmie's career with the company. There had been some well thought out and executed graphics on his card and a presentation of a television set was made adding

> *"All of it comes with our warmest wishes for a long and happy retirement, and the hope that it will dawn on you for the first time, that there can be fun otherwise than working on the Electrical Times"*

Ken finished with a toast for a long and happy retirement to Jimmie and Nancy.

After the farewell party he returned to his office for one last time picked up his briefcase and with almost no backward glance, retired.

Chapter 21   Outside Work & Retirement

Outside of his work and family two interests occupied his time. Freemasonry seemed to occupy some of his time and then especially during the November period of remembrance was the gathering of the boys of the 49th Recce.

His interest in the Freemasons started when he was thirty-six years old. It was one of his colleagues at work that encouraged him to come along to one of their social functions so that he could see for himself what was involved. He went along as a guest to the next social function and found that it wasn't the conspiratorial society that he had heard rumoured. It was a voluntary organisation that traced its origins back to the local fraternities of stonemasons who from the end of the fourteenth century formed what today might be called a union to look after the well being of other stonemasons. It was not a religion but the members had to believe in an Almighty Creator and practise a religion. The members, all male in those days, were like minded who had to be of good character and reputation.

The lodge that he was considering joining was called Con Amore which literally translated meant 'with love' and to distinguish it from any other Lodge of the same name it was numbered 3633. Their meetings took place on the last Thursday of the month. At that time meetings were held in the Piccadilly Hotel that looked out at Eros who in turn looked down on those with assignations gathered below. The meetings were at a convenient time for him to go straight from work. It was a short walk of less than a mile from Sardinia Street, crossing over Kingsway and then down Long Acre to Piccadilly Circus. In the winter or on less weather inviting evenings he could catch the tube from Holborn to Piccadilly Circus or perhaps take a cab.

The onus was on Jimmie to take the initiative and ask to become a member as it was not the correct protocol to invite candidates. After further talks with his work colleague and a couple of other Lodge members Jimmie submitted his application. The application was duly received and Jimmie was called for an interview. After the interview and a simple Lodge ballot he was accepted.

His journey began on the 26th February 1953, he started his first of three degrees when he was initiated as an Apprentice. During the ceremony of initiation Jimmie undertook to fulfil certain obligations as a Mason by swearing on the Bible. He was then progressively taught the meanings of the symbols of Freemasonry and entrusted with grips, signs and words to signify to other members that he has been so initiated. The degrees are part allegorical morality play and part lecture. In the course of the three degrees, he would promise to keep the secrets associated with his degree from lower degrees and outsiders and to support a fellow Mason in distress as much as he could within the law.

He worked hard, learning the allegories, illustrated by symbols which were mainly, but not exclusively, drawn from the stonemason's tools – the square and compasses, the level and plumb rule, the trowel, the rough and smooth ashlars, among others. Moral lessons are attributed to each of these tools,

By November he was able to progress to the next degree, that of Journeyman where he extended his knowledge of Masonry.

The following October 28th at the age of thirty-seven he was Raised to the final status of Master Mason at which stage he had been entrusted with the passwords, signs and secret handshakes which to the day he died he kept secret.

When he had passed his third degree he was free to fully join in with the activities of the lodge be these charitable religious or social. He looked upon it not as a job achievement route but as a way of releasing the tensions of work. That last Thursday of every month gave him the opportunity to mix with his fellows and afterwards some would leave the Piccadilly Hotel and cross the Circus into the clubs of Soho where they could eat drink and relax. Sometimes there were occasions when a separate room and coffee was provided to enable them to normalise.

After being active in the Lodge for fourteen years in 1967 he became Master of the Lodge a status that he felt very privileged to hold. Apart from the usual commerciality of running the Lodge he introduced the tradition of a toast "to Con Amore Lodge 3633" every time they dined after a Lodge meeting. He also had to organise the social end of year gathering of Ladies Night or the Master's Ball. For his year he chose to have it at Quaglinos an Italian restaurant situated in the basement of St James's Palace Hotel on Bury Street.

Quaglino's was founded by Giovanni Quaglino in 1929, with his brother Ernest as headwaiter. The restaurant was highly popular with the British establishment from the 1930s through the 1950s and was a favourite haunt of London's café society which included many royals and on one occasion Queen Elizabeth II dined there. On these occasions besides all the usual speeches it was expected that the Master's wife would also make a short speech. The thought of having to stand up in front of two hundred people and talk frightened Nancy. Jimmie, besides working on his speech helped Nancy to write and prepare herself. On the night of the Ball they were collected from home by car and delivered to the door of the restaurant to be welcomed by the perfect greeter. Nancy's nervousness started to rise as the meal progressed and by the time the desert had been served and the coffee started she knew that her time was rapidly approaching.

The speeches started. Her nerves broke and she left the table for the Powder Room. Unfortunately Jimmie who could not leave the table had to watch her go knowing full well what must have been going on in her mind. Shortly Peter went to find her to see how she was. Still nervous but calmer than before, she was reassured that everyone understood her situation and would in no way be critical, she accompanied Peter back to her seat next to Jimmie at the head table. Jimmie provided a gentle invitation to her and with only a little nervousness showing her talk was received with a round of applause. A much relieved Nancy was then able to relax and enjoy the dancing and the rest of the evening.

His Grand year completed he continued his involvement with the Lodge and in 1980 was awarded the Grand Rank a position that he held until he died. This award happened at the same time that the ET moved to the London Suburb of Sutton. There was no easy walk across London to the meeting venue anymore, so he travelled up by car. In 1986 Con Amore moved its meeting venue to the Park Court Hotel, Lancaster Gate. This gave Jimmie yet another problem. Car parking at a new location. It was on a wet autumnal evening, the last Thursday in the month and Jimmie was hunting the area near Lancaster Gate for a Parking space. He managed to find an automatic parking car park. Not fully appreciating what this meant he drove in, collected his ticket, moved away from the ticket machine to try and work out which way he should drive. The next thing he knew was that events were taken out of his control. The car started to move. He pulled on the hand brake but to no avail. Then he appeared to be in a large black void going he knew not where. Panic. He sounded his horn flashed his lights in an attempt to get attention from someone somewhere to stop his journey into hell. After a short time that to Jimmie seemed an eternity the car returned to where it had started and a fluorescent jacketed parking assistant was there to explain what "automatic parking" meant in practice. Jimmie made it to the Lodge and found another car park for the next time.

His family's concerns that after nearly fifty years at work, essentially for the same journal, he would find retirement difficult were unfounded, instead he enjoyed the release from the pressures of work. He found that he had the time to devote to become the secretary of the Lodge. He changed Lynda's small bedroom at the front of the house over the entrance doorway into an office. Desk and a chair, there was to be no word processor or computer it was to be as had been the case at work, what he knew best, a typewriter although he did succumb to a small electric version. All his hard effort was appreciated by his fellow brothers as he was thought of as

> *"a great and very efficient secretary.......*
> *...a most highly respected friend and*
> *brother."*

It was in 1984 just after Peter had moved into a large house in Kingswood Warren and Jimmie had been volunteered to paint a six and a half metre double garage door with a 50 mm paintbrush that his breathing problems were noticed heralding the start of COPD. He had stopped cigarette smoking but he still clung to his pipe. But no more since his breathing got worse and he was diagnosed with Emphysema, a lung disease where the air sacs in the lungs are damaged and over time, the inner walls of the air sacs weaken and rupture — creating larger air spaces instead of many small ones. It is not a very nice feeling being breathless and Jimmie had to learn how to control the panic that ensued.

In 1986 he changed the large company car for one of a more reasonable size opting for the top of the range Austin-Rover Maestro 1.6 HL with electric windows that he thought were great fun. It was an automatic, the first automatic that he had ever owned or driven. He was obviously proud of the automatic that he had an "Automatic" badge added to the manufacturer's model decal on the rear of the car.

Sadly in April of the following year just before his 70th birthday he received news that his elder sister Phyllis had died of a heart attack.

1989 was now approaching, his golden wedding anniversary year. To celebrate the occasion he organised a dinner dance at the Bridge House Hotel at the top of Reigate hill. The bridge house restaurant had a small dance floor and live music to get you in the rhythm, the music genre changed throughout the week. Fortunately the 15th of September, a Friday it was dance band night ideally suitable for his generation. He chose a multi-choice menu of his liking and arranged with the maître d' for un-priced copies of the menu to be provided for his guests. Friday night arrived and the extended family together with his work colleague and friend Ken Pounds with his wife Audrey gathered and the evening began. With the excuse that he was just going to check that the table was ready he had a quick look to confirm that the menus were as requested. All was well. The wine flowed and the gastric juices were actively satisfied and then came the desert. The waiter floated around the table offering menus from which to choose the desert. Jimmie looked at his menu then looked across at Peter and with his fingers made as a gun fired it into his head. The menus were priced. The words of Robbie Burns to a mouse came to mind – "The best laid schemes o' Mice an' Men, gang aft agley."

Whilst he was living in Cottenham Park, every Remembrance Sunday he would walk up to the War Memorial on Wimbledon Common following in the tradition set by his father to attend the service and watch the parade. There he would meet some of his 1939 TA friends and remember those who did not return. No doubt after the service, he and the other attending survivors would retire to a local hostelry and raise a glass to their fallen comrades and perhaps to themselves as well.

On the 30th April 1950 there was a memorial service at St Martin in the Fields, London, when a table bearing the Corps Badge and a Book of Remembrance containing the Corps Roll of Honour was dedicated. The table and book were not to remain at that church; they were later to be entrusted to the Reverend PTB "Tubby" Clayton MC of All Hallows-by-the-Tower, on Byward Street. All Hallows is most probably the oldest church in the City of London. It survived the great fire of London and although badly damaged in the Blitz it had been extensively reconstructed and was rededicated in 1957. Tubby was responsible for starting Toc H, now an international Christian organisation. It was started during the First World War at a house named Toc H on Gasthuisstraat in Poperinge, Belgium as a soldier's club where all were equal as indicated by the sign at the entrance "All rank abandon, ye who enter here." Tubby's association with the military made him approachable with regard to providing a permanent home for the table and Roll of Honour. He agreed to the request and Sir Bernard Paget Colonel-Commandant of the Corps entrusted Rev Clayton with the table and Corps Roll of Honour to remain permanently in the Baptistery of All Hallows by the Tower.

The association of All Hallows with the 25th Recce Regiments continued and a remembrance service was held in the afternoon on Remembrance Sunday. During that service representatives of the Recce Regiments were invited to lay wreaths in the Baptistry and at one particular service on the 10th November 1985 a stained glass window bearing the Corps Badge was dedicated.

Times change and old soldiers fade away or move to pastures green as happened with Jimmie. In 1953 his move to Grand Drive I believe brought about a change in the way he remembered in November. It must have been about this time or shortly afterwards that he rekindled his association with a group of old soldiers, Polar Bears, with whom he had fought alongside; the 49th Recce. They under the guise of the Old Comrades Association gathered at the Union Jack Club close to Waterloo Station and Jimmie joined them.

One day in 1983 a letter addressed to the Old Comrades Association, was delivered to the Union Jack Club. In the customary top right-hand corner of the envelope were the stamps. They bore the image of a queen but not our Queen's head, it was that of another queen together with the wording "Nederland".

Chapter 22   Liberators Recall

Meanwhile back in Holland. The gun that had been removed by the Pulles from Sergeant Mould's armoured car long ago in August 1945 was still resting in their garden. In 1979 a neighbour asked if Maarten Pulle, the son of Reinier Pulle, who was then living at de Looijenboom if he knew from what vehicle the gun had been liberated. Maarten did not know and could not answer the simple question. The challenge was there, he had to find out and so a lot of research started. The first thing that he tried was to place a request in the local newspaper asking the local residents if they had any knowledge about the liberation and in particular about Sergeant Mould's car. There were many replies and all indicated that the Canadians were involved as they had liberated Apeldoorn just to the north of Loenen. There was also the mention of "Polar Bears" and as polar bears lived in the Arctic North they thought it was also a connection to the Canadians. Mr Pulle then wrote making enquiries of the Canadian Army. In their reply the Canadians acknowledged that they had been part of Montgomery's left flank, which involved the liberation of parts of Holland, they could find no record of any of their units liberating the town of Loenen in Gelderland. By 1980 Maarten concluded that it was not the Canadians that liberated the village. From other information that had been gathered, he now believed that it was a British unit called the 49th (West Riding) Reconnaissance Regiment, Royal Armoured Corps that had driven into Loenen in April 1945. The neighbour's question still remained unanswered.

It was now nearly forty years that this private memorial had resided in the garden of "de Looijenboom". Mr Frederick Pulle, his brother Maarten and his family thought that it would be an idea to use the gun as a memorial in the village centre and make its dedication part of the celebrations for the upcoming (39th) anniversary of their liberation.

Another article was placed in the local paper seeking the opinion of the residents of Loenen about Pulle's idea of using the gun as a monument, a memorial of the war. To his delight the people responded most enthusiastically. Pulle then put forward his proposals to the Council. As part of the plans he wanted to mention the crew of the armoured car by name. Here again he made some enquiries but his efforts were unsuccessful. The Council were also keen not only to just mention the names but thought it a good idea to invite any surviving soldiers that liberated their town to come to Loenen to join with them in the celebrations.

With his enquiries drawing a blank and the clock ticking down Maarten decided on one way that might bring a solution was to visit York the principal town of the West Ridings. In the spring of 1983 Pulle set out for Yorkshire to see what he could find out. In York he visited the main library and found a book about the role of the Yorkshire Regiments in WW2. Inside the book Pulle found a photograph of the Humber Mark IV armoured car with the polar bear on the left mudguard and 41 on the right mudguard. This was the closest he had reached for an answer to his research but where did he have to go to now? There is an old saying 'if you want to know ask a policeman'. This was exactly what Maarten did. The policeman was unable to help directly but he did point Maarten in the direction of the Head Quarters of 2nd Infantry Division which was based in the Imphal Barracks at Fulford along the A19 on the south side of York.

The next morning from his hotel in the city centre he caught the number 415 bus to travel the one and a half miles to the Imphal Barracks. On his arrival he spoke to a couple of officers who alas had no answer to the question posed. Pulle felt a bit downhearted but the officers were so impressed by the story and the effort that had been expended so far that they promised to try and find the answer. They couldn't do it immediately but asked

Maarten if could return next week when they would have some information for him. On his return a week later true to their promise they had the information for him, which they hoped would prove useful. They gave him the name and contact details of Captain Ken Baker who was the President of the 49th West Riding Regimental Association. Unfortunately the address was not local but in London so he returned to Holland. Immediately on his return a letter went off to Captain Baker who in his reply was able to tell Maarten that it was an armoured car from "C" Squadron driven by Sergeant Wilf Mould that had arrived in Loenen in 1945.

Maarten explained to Ken what the Council in Loenen had proposed and extended an invitation on their behalf. It was their wish for the Old Comrades of the 49th Recce and their wives or partner's to come to Loenen for the unveiling of the memorial in their town centre and to partake with them in the anniversary of their liberation celebrations. The invitation was enthusiastically accepted by Captain Baker who then started to organise things at his end whilst Maarten found that his work in Loenen had only just begun.

Maarten formed a committee with himself as chairman and Mr Paul Sanders as secretary. They were joined by Mrs Wilma Voskamp, secretary, Jan van Putten, treasurer, Henk Berends, Hendrik Reusken and Gerrit van de Sprenge. The choice of the members ensured that they represented the most important associations of their village. It had the responsibility for organising the erection of the monument and all that was entailed for the visit by the veterans.

They chose Saturday 14 April 1984 as the day for unveiling the monument, which with all the work that had to be done was not that far away. Having settled the date the next thing that had to decide was where to position the monument. The village had just finished building their Civic

Centre. It was a proud achievement. They had raised all the funding within the village and it had been built using the skills and labour of volunteer villagers. It stood in the newer part of Loenen, which would not have been there in 1945. It was a modern building set in an open space with a large tree denoting the corner of the plot at a road junction. A tree it seemed was to play another significant part in the historic decisions of the village. In the winter of 1983/4 the tree succumbed to the strong winds of a storm and came crashing down across the road. An omen one might argue and as a tree across the road led to the obtaining of the gun so another tree led to marking the spot for the memorial.

On Wednesday night Jimmie and Nancy excitedly packed their cases and on the 12th April left Raynes Park for the assembly point at the Union Jack Club. Thirty veterans including Sergeant Mould and Major Judge together with their wives and their cases ensconced themselves in a coach supplied by Windsorian. They set out on a journey that this time would take them until Friday afternoon, a mere 24 hours, to arrive in Loenen rather than the dangerous ten months it took them from July 1944. They spent the night in the Belgium town of Bruges no doubt sampling the local beers and chocolate that the town had to offer. The next day in the early afternoon they arrived on time in Loenen. The coach was met by Paul Sanders and directed into a parking space beside the Cafe Zaal on Beekbergerweg where they were given refreshments and a warm welcome. Afterwards they were introduced to the locals who had agreed to share their homes with them during the visit. Jimmie and Nancy were greeted by their hosts for the next two days a Mr and Mrs de Winter-Meth. They accompanied them to their house which was not far away off Hoofdweg. After settling themselves into their room and a wash to clear away the tiredness of the journey they joined the de Winter-Meths for a meal complemented by a pleasant wine and mixed with many tales of now and then. They talked until it was time for an early night for not only had it been a long day but it was going to be even longer on Saturday.

The long awaited and planned for Saturday morning of 14th April had arrived. To say there weren't nerves would be a lie, this was the day the Pulles had worked for three years to achieve. The time had passed for further rehearsals, their hard work and planning had been done and now the proof of the pudding was to be sampled. The Pulle brothers were getting ready in de Looijenboom Maarten with his speech safely in his pocket; the scroll containing the change of ownership detail was ready for Maarten's grandson to look after and soon it would be off to De Brink.

On the other side of Loenen at the far end of Hoofdweg another family were getting ready, that of Paul and Elizabeth Sanders. He too had helped in the planning of this day and how smoothly it goes depended on him. He was the Master of Ceremonies; he had to make certain all the right people were in the right place at the right time. He knew that they have all done their homework and in a few minutes the months of preparation would be put to the test. Whilst the veterans were enjoying their breakfasts Paul headed off to De Brink.

In a house in Droefakkers Mr and Mrs Dorland were ensuring that Wilf Mould and his wife Angela were enjoying a quiet breakfast. For Wilf it was going to be a long day, as he was one of the main characters of 1945 as well as today since it was his car's gun that was being unveiled.

Just down the road from De Brink Mr and Mrs de Winter-Meths are stoking up Jimmie's inner man with a typical Dutch breakfast. His day was going to be one of no responsibilities he was there like the rest of the veterans to enjoy and celebrate the occasion with the locals. Suitably booted and suited in his Sunday best he followed the orders of the day that 'Medals were to be worn' he proudly pinned his five well deserved medals to the left breast of his jacket.

1939-45 Star *was awarded for service in the campaign of at least 28 days service.*
It is a six pointed star struck in yellow copper zinc alloy to fit in a 44 mm diameter circle. It had a central design of the Royal Cypher "GRI VI", surmounted by a crown and is inscribed "THE 1939–1945 STAR". The ribbon is 32 mm wide of three equal stripes of Naval Dark blue, Army red and RAF light blue.

France and Germany Star *was awarded to those that fought in North East Europe.*
It is a six pointed star struck in yellow copper zinc alloy to fit in a 44 mm diameter circle. It had a central design of the Royal Cypher "GRI VI", surmounted by a crown and is inscribed "THE FRANCE AND GERMANY STAR" The ribbon is 32 millimetres wide, with equal width dark blue, white, red, white and dark blue bands. The colours are those of the Union flag and also the national colours of France and the Netherlands.

Defence Medal *was awarded for at least three years service. It is a disk, 36 millimetres in diameter struck in cupro-nickel. It shows the bareheaded effigy of King George VI around the perimeter is the legend "GEORGIVS VI D:G:BR:OMN:REX F:D:IND: IMP.".*
The ribbon is 32 millimetres wide, with a 4½ millimetres wide green band, a 1-millimetre wide black band and a 4½ millimetres wide

green band, repeated and separated by a 12 millimetres wide orange band. The flame-coloured orange centre band and the green bands symbolise enemy attacks on Britain's green and pleasant land while the narrow black bands represent the black-outs against air attacks.

War Medal was awarded for at least 28 days service. It is a disk, 36 millimetres in diameter struck in cupro-nickel, It shows the crowned effigy of King George VI, facing left around the perimeter is the legend "GEORGIVS VI D:G:BR:OMN:REX ET INDIAE IMP:". The ribbon is 32 millimetres wide, with a 6½ millimetres wide red band, a 6½ millimetres wide blue band and a 2 millimetres wide white band, repeated in reverse order and separated by a 2 millimetres wide red band. The colours are those of the British Union Jack.

Territorial Efficiency Medal and bar was awarded for twelve years of efficient service plus another 6 years to earn the bar. The medal was struck in silver and is oval, 39 millimetres high and 32 millimetres wide. It shows the crowned effigy of King George VI, facing left around the perimeter is "GEORGIVS VI D G BR OMN REX ET INDIÆ IMP". The ribbon is 32 mm wide of dark green, edged with 3 millimetres wide lime-yellow bands.

Separately Jimmie also wore the
Kings Badge for loyal service.

The clock ticked towards the assembly hour so with his pocket-sized point and shoot camera in hand they walked the short distance along Hoofdweg to De Brink, the Civic Centre. A long day with many surprises was about to begin.

He could hear the band before he saw it, then as he rounded the bend the white-topped caps and dark blue uniforms of the band could be seen in the far corner of the entrance plaza. The camera came out and the point and shoot started its day's work.

In total 30 veterans had answered the call not just the surviving crew of Crusader. Together with their wives and the invited guests of Loenen the party swelled to well over 100 people.

There was time to meet and greet in the hall with a cup of tea or coffee and a biscuit or two. In the meantime the excited local girl scouts assembled outside. The band had stopped to take a short break but over the general hubbub of chat that was not noticed. Then the call came for the veterans to be on parade and form up outside. Once they were in position the wives and guests were invited to follow.

The scene was now set. The covered memorial was in the south eastern corner. The dais complete with lectern was to its immediate left. The dignitaries representing Loenen and Apeldoorn stood to the left of the dais next to the building. Next was a line of girl scouts in their orange tops that stood along the wall of the main hall. Then came the guests standing behind the flag pole and finally facing down towards the dais and monument stood the veterans. All along the adjacent road the locals had gathered. However, there were two veterans of the main cast missing, Major Judge and Sergeant Mould were nowhere to be seen. They heard the band start, the sound came from behind, it was a March. A heavy engine vehicle could be heard coming down the road then a sound familiar to

Jimmie could be heard, that of a Rootes 6 cyl 90 hp petrol engine. He turned to look behind him and there coming down the road was a MkIV Humber Heavy armoured car with a Polar Bear emblem on the left-hand wing and the number 41 on a diagonal split green and gold square on the right-wing. Sitting atop were the missing veterans, Judge and Mould with Mould in the commander's position. The car stopped behind the dignitaries and the two veterans displayed that their agility to get out and off the car had not diminished over the past thirty-nine years.

The official ceremony started with Mr Maarten Pulle's grandson delivering to him the scroll transferring the ownership of the gun from the Pulle Family to the Village Council. Mr Maarten Pulle then presented the scroll to Mrs Marietje Berends who was president of the Loenen Liaison Association with the Municipality of Apeldoorn saying

> *"..... I sincerely hope that this monument will stay here for many years to come as a remembrance to our liberation and a token of our thankfulness to the British Soldiers that fought for our freedom."*

Mrs Berends accepted it on behalf of the People of Loenen. She added her thanks to the Polar Bears that had liberated the village and went on to liberate Holland.

Major Harry Judge was invited to respond on behalf of the 49th Recce.

> *" Ladies and gentlemen. I'm sorry that I can't speak to you in Dutch but as many of you have probably realised for a long time that for over a thousand years my fellow countryman have firmly believed that God speaks English and somewhat arrogantly have never*

bothered accordingly to learn any other language but their own.........

In April 1945 almost to the day the men who are here from England today had the privilege of playing a little part in the liberation of Holland in general and Loenen in particular. I am also happy to say that the gentleman who drove the first vehicle to appear and of which that gun is a part, in spite of having his vehicle destroyed, is still alive and fit, even if he is 39 years older than he was........."

The gentleman to which Major Harry Judge referred was Sergeant Wilf Mould, the same person who 40 years before had found Jimmie by the roadside near Maasbree and by his action in calling for medical attention Jimmie believed had saved his life.

The great moment had arrived. Major Judge on completing his speech moved over to the cord tied to the corner of the drape covering the gun and preceded slowly and in a dignified way pulled the drape off the gun unveiling the monument.

Ken Baker then came forward and presented the Union Jack to the girl scouts who with help prepared and raised it to half mast. Captain Ken Baker, who had been second in command of "C" Squadron, had missed the liberation in 1945. He had been captured after being severely injured on The Island and at the time of the liberation was lying as a POW in the hospital at Apeldoorn just ten kilometres to the north.

Sergeant Mould who had not lost any of the sharpness of the parade ground stepped forward and laid a poppy wreath at the base of the new monument. After a moment or two of reflection he turned and went back in line. The quiet that had descended was then broken by a single bugler playing the Last Post followed by one minute's silence. At the end of the silence Mr Sanders walked forward and escorted a blind veteran Mr Granville Waterworth who was on the arm of a girl guide to the dais where he recited The Exhortation.

Sergeant Mould came forward once again, this time to the flagpole and whilst the British National Anthem was being played raised the union jack slowly to full mast with the flag arriving at the top as the first verse finished. As is the tradition in Holland they always play two verses which test the memories of most Brits as they usually only play the first verse at home. (It is worth remembering so that you can come prepared to save the embarrassment of having to mime the second verse.)

As the strains of the second verse of the National Anthem died away Mr Henk Berends one of the organising committee members raised the Dutch flag whilst their National Anthem was played.

It was then the turn of Major Beelands van Blokland the representative of the Municipality of Apeldoorn to take centre stage. He started by placing a time capsule in the barrel of the gun. The time capsule included the names and signatures of "C" Squadron's Commander Major Harry Judge and Sergeant Wilfred Mould the driver of the armoured car. Added to those were various signatures of the old Polar Bears, their widows, and wives who were present at the opening of the monument of which Jimmie and Nancy were two. Also included were the signatures of a selection of the Dutch who were present. Major Beelands van Blokland then sealed the gun barrel and left the time capsule waiting in the dark for another generation to discover.

Mr Beelands van Blokland then made his formal address which contrary to the rest of the Dutch speakers started in Dutch followed by English. He started by expressing his personal thanks to his liberators for what they did in 1945 against an enemy who he described as one that:-

> *"....oppresses beyond human limits and human scope. They stole our goods, cars, horses even bikes. With each year getting worser and worser.............."*

After giving further examples of how the Dutch were treated by the Nazis he concluded with further praise and a thank you to the liberators. Afterwards he laid a wreath on behalf of the Dutch People to join that of the 49th Recces at the base of the monument.

Mr Maarten Pulle then brought the ceremony to its conclusion with a final tribute and thanks to the 49th. The band started to play and Jimmie was only too keen to take Nancy to have a look at the thirteen tons of armoured plate that had been his home during his time in Europe, explaining to her his normal position and where he was on that day in November. They also looked at the memorial which had a plate set into the base inscribed in Dutch saying

> *Remembrance at the liberation of Loenen Veluwe*
> *on April 16, 1946 by the*
> *49th (West Riding) Reconnaissance Regiment*

The following year on the fortieth anniversary of their liberation a separate memorial was unveiled during a ceremony on 17th April 1995 which read as follows

> *In memory of the people of Loenen*
> *who passed away*
> *in the years 1940 - 1945*

After all the hard work of the Pulle family together with the people of Loenen the gun from the Armoured car "Crusader" driven by Sgt Mould W. is now the Polar Bear's Monument in their village of Loenen in the municipality of Apeldoorn that "C" Squadron liberated in April of 1945.

The day was not over for after a period to look at the car and the memorial together with a comfort break it was time for another treat. He had heard the name "Keep them Rolling" mentioned and that afternoon he was to understand what it meant.

Waiting for them in the field behind De Brink was an assortment of ex-World War 2 army vehicles. There were jeeps, open back troop carriers, closed in lorries, trailers even a fuel tanker. It wasn't to be a static show they were asked to get on board and once settled down they went off in convoy. The suspension left a lot to be desired and certainly was stiffer than memory permitted. They wound their way through the local countryside and stopped to look at the site of another memorial. This time it was to an RAF Spitfire pilot that had been shot down fighting to help liberate Holland. The convoy then moved on to a local woodland setting where refreshments were provided. It was whilst in that setting Jimmie's imagination took him back forty years to the days and nights that as young soldiers they would be encamped in similar surroundings brewing up and having a meal. And through his eyes, as every older generation will know, he saw himself not as a retired man but still as a young soldier.

Sunday saw church parade at 10.45. During the service thanks and tributes were paid to not only those veterans present but also to those whose names made up the Roll of Honour and to those that suffered long and perhaps non-recoverable injuries. At 11.40 from inside the church they could hear the symbolic ringing of the liberation bells from the tower above them.

After the service it was a return to the civic centre this time for a photocall before the final piece of free time to enjoy the environment that by their efforts forty years ago the Dutch have succeeded in making. For tomorrow morning the Windsorian coach will whisk them away back home to England.

In memory of the English who gave their lives for the liberation of Holland and especially their village the Union Jack is flown in front of De Brink at half mast on Remembrance Sunday in November. As a sign of thanks to all that took part in the liberation the flag is proudly flown at full mast in May, the anniversary of Holland's liberation.

In the following years some of the veterans returned, the numbers dwindling until all the old soldiers had faded away. Now, at the memorial that to some means so much, it is their sons and grandsons that remember them and their heroic efforts. Jimmie's son Peter and grandsons Christopher and Simon with his children remember and are gratified that the residents are still thankful for the sacrifices of those old soldiers. Paul Sander's in his parting message to them after one particular visit to the memorial clearly indicated the deep gratitude that is felt by the Dutch,

> *"Please remember what your father did, and Grandfather did for the Netherlands and thank you for liberating the Netherlands, for your part in the liberation. Thank you very much."*

Mould & Judge Arrive in a MkIV

Nancy, Jimmie & Angela Mould

Peter's Quest for the Gun is Over

Chapter 23   The Sun Sets

Jimmie never did return to either Caledon or Loenen either distance or ill health got in the way. He did continue to attend the remembrance services but a time came as the numbers dwindled when old soldiers faded away, that he too found with his worsening breathing that he could no longer go. Instead he chose to do his remembering from his chair whilst watching the Remembrance service on the television.

The rest of the '80s passed and in came the 90's. Not only did the 90's bring to an end the 20th Century they also heralded some good times and some not so good. It was to be the decade for the final chapter of the remaining members of our Polar Bear's original family.

In October 1990 following in his great grandfather's and his grandfather's footsteps Christopher, in the Combined Cadet Force at his public school, obtained the rank of CSM. It was a proud moment for him as he commanded the Guard of Honour at the annual inspection in the presence of his Grandfather and Father. Then the first sadness of the decade for in 1991 his baby sister Olive at only seventy-two years old had a fatal heart attack just before Christmas. This followed with more sadness as only four years later in 1995 that his eldest sister Dorothy died leaving our Jimmie the sole remaining member of that family.

Christopher brought more happiness into his life with an invitation to his marriage to Alice on 15th June 1996 at St Leonards Church in Denton near New Haven and afterwards at the Grand Hotel in Eastbourne. Christopher was the first of his grandchildren to get married.

In 1997 he celebrated his 80th birthday with a family dinner, unfortunately because of personal circumstances Peter was unable to attend.

The Sun Sets

As the seasons of 1998 passed so did the autumn of his life pass into winter and as his body failed Nancy came to the hard decision that she could no longer care for him at home. In November he was taken into St Helier Hospital with renal failure. Shortly afterwards Nancy also became hospitalised and joined him in the same hospital. Although they were two floors apart the nurses kindly took her to visit him on several occasions, one of those being Christmas Day. On the 31st December the sun set for the last time on the penultimate year of the Twentieth Century, for Jimmie it was never to rise again. The whole cast of 68 Pepys Road had gone.

Within two weeks his wife of nearly sixty years, after appearing to recover well had a bad stroke from which she was not to recover and on the 16th January joined him.

Near the wind chimes of other people's outward signs of grief and remembrance, on a damp morning on the 8th March 1999 his ashes mixed together with those of his wife, now inseparable in death as they were in life, were laid to rest by Peter and Simon in the cemetery that occupies the fields in which he once played as a boy.

To a Polar Bear we say thank you and may your God bless you.

Polar Bear Memorial at Maasbree

Polar Bear Memorial in Loenen

Epilogue

Thanks initially to R J C Pulle and Confuzzled then many others on the way I would not have been able to tell the tale. In April 2008 I was able to visit both Loenen and Maasbree with my elder son Christopher and repeat the same the following year with my other son Simon. It was a great thrill for me to travel with them across France, Belgium and Holland tracing the Footsteps of a Polar Bear, our Polar Bear! Accompanied by my wife on the 6th May 2015 I revisited the grave of my Father's driver Cecil Kirby in the cemetery at Maasbree. The cemetery is the local Roman Catholic cemetery lying to the east of the town on a little brick-paved road called Achter de Hoven. There are six Commonwealth Soldiers graves at the end of a tree-lined path from the main entrance. Of those six there rest four members of "C" Squadron of the 49th RECCE, my Father's driver being one of them. To the left as you pass through the main entrance is a small chapel. That day I chose to leave a short note in the Memorial book saying:-

> *Visiting C.E.Kirby*
> *Driver of my Father's Armoured car*
> *Killed on 23 November 1944.*
> *My Father was also seriously injured*
> *at the same time.*
> *He died in 1998.*

Completing the entry I added my name and email address.

On the notice board over the lectern holding the book were the name, address and telephone number of a local called Ton Boots with a note indicating he had an interest in the Polar Bears. I tried phoning him but without success. On my return to the UK I wrote to him and another new friendship with the Dutch was started.

Slowly over the years the old soldiers faded away being furloughed to that parade ground or battlefield elsewhere.

After the war Major Harry Judge returned to teaching becoming the second master at the Elms Prep School at Colwall, near Malvern. There he taught English, French and rugby with a commanding officers firm but benevolent authority and became well liked by his charges. Having been presented with two pigs by his father in law, which promptly ran riot in Bromsgrove high street during the rush hour, he made pigs and soft fruit farming a second string to his bow, farming thirty acres. He gained an enduring affection for pigs as they, he observed, possessed many of the virtues of little boys without all the vices and any troublesome ones could always, unlike little boys, be sent to the abattoir. He remained at the school until he retired in 1979 then he took up after dinner speaking. After the death of his wife Beryl Tomey in 1979 he subsequently married Noel Dyson a talented actress with many credits for appearances in popular television programmes and found himself in the entirely different world of the thespian set. In 1984 he attended the unveiling ceremony of the "gun" in Loenen and the subsequent year led a parade of soldiers through the streets of Utrecht to celebrate the 50th anniversary of the end of the war. Unfortunately his eyesight was failing with age and by the time he was 90 he was blind although that did not change his zest for life. His furlough started on 13th December 2003 leaving behind his two sons from his first marriage.

Sid Godfrey the man who helped me the most to meet and subsequently join in the activities of the 49th Recce Polar Bears was to fade away. He was notified that he had been awarded France's highest order of merit, the Légion d'honneur. Unfortunately on 18th April 2015 his furlough came through before it arrived. It is now proudly worn on the left breast by his son Michael whenever he represents his father.

Wilf Mould retired with his wife to his house called Beggars Roost in Sutton on Sea, Lincolnshire. One day he went out to get some provisions from the local supermarket and on his return home was mugged by a group of youths. He suffered some physical damage from which he never really fully recovered. Angela was cross, to put it mildly, for she said that had it not been for Wilf's efforts during the war these youths would not be enjoying the freedom that they had abused when they struck him down. All for what, she queried, they reaped no reward. A year or so later another old soldier faded away.

To the best of my knowledge Joe Hoadley was the last of the band of Polar Bears that met at the Union Jack Club. In 2017 he also received the red ribboned medal from France, the Légion d'honneur, unlike Sid Godfrey he was able to pin it to his breast before the 25th of August 2018 when he got his calling. Anybody that knew Joe also knew that wherever he went his harmonica went too. At any opportunity he would serenade the gathering usually with the old Vera Lyn classics. For those that went to his funeral service they thought that this would be the first time in Joe's presence when the harmonica would not be played. How wrong they were. A smile did cross my face when during the service we were serenaded by a recording of Joe playing his harmonica.

In April 2016 my wife and I returned for a couple of days to Loenen on the anniversary of their liberation and included in that trip a chance to travel down to Maasbree to put faces to the names of Ton and his partner Wil.

The early summer sun shone from a clear blue sky into our conservatory. Sunday roast had been consumed and a general feeling of satisfied relaxation was the order of the afternoon. The peace was broken by the ring of the phone. I answered it not knowing what to expect. After confirming that I was Peter Knox the caller introduced himself as Lee Smith the grandson of Cecil Kirby, my Father's armoured car driver. From all those years ago my message in the chapel at the Maasbree Cemetery has borne fruit.

A meeting with Lee followed in July of that year and in April of 2018 Lee and his wife Debbie joined Pat and me in a visit to his grandfather's grave in Maasbree. History gets fascinating especially when it's personal and on this occasion even more so. Not only did we meet Jo Duijf the witness of the incidences involving Cecil Kirby and my Father he also showed us where they had happened. We also met the maternal Grandson, Peter Wilms, of the owner of the farm in which they had both spent their last night together.

The 75th anniversary of Maasbree's liberation was in November 2019 and together with my wife and sons Christopher and Simon we returned to join in with their celebrations. We were joined by Lee and Debbie who were accompanied on this occasion by his stepfather Raymond Duralski and his sister Camille Duralski, and his sister Camille Duralski who had travelled from America. This was obviously a very special time for them all, made even more poignant for Lee, as with him he brought some of his mother's ashes and in their own private and solemn ceremony were able to reunite her with her father.

I was honoured by being asked to join in with their liberation celebrations on 23rd November by making an address at the graveside of the fallen. We assembled at 09.45 hrs on the square outside the church the procession was led by the Saint Martin Civic Guard their colours aloft. Following them was the Marching Band Aldegondis and next was the Maasbree Male Voice Choir. Bringing up the rear was the Lady Mayor Mrs Delisson with Alderman Hermans and members of the organising committee together with us, the British contingent. At 10.00 hrs the band struck up and we stepped off to the cemetery. As we approached the graves the band peeled off to the right to stand facing the graves and the choir to the left. I followed the Mayor and Alderman to a small lectern to one side of the graves.

Whilst the Lady Mayor was making her contribution in Dutch welcoming the various participants and continuing with a brief reflection on 75 years ago I looked to my left. Beyond the graves, beyond the band, beyond the cemetery wall to the trees and fields, to a once upon a time track road called Rozendaal. I reflected that 75 years ago almost to the minute Lee's grandfather, Cecil Kirby, was lying beside the road his war over and two kilometres further on my Father was also laid beside the road unconscious believed to be dead.

The Lady Mayor had finished and now it was my turn to step forward for my five minutes of fame. I moved to the lectern, looked around the gathering of the old through to the young. They were all here to pay tribute and give their thanks to the boys of '44 of which my father was one. My notes were in my pocket and I was resolute that is where they would stay I was not going to let him down and so from my heart and my head I began –

> *Lady Mayor, Alderman Hermans, the Liberated people of Maasbree and the relatives of the Liberators may I say how privileged I feel being here with you today.*
>
> *75 years ago on the evening of Wednesday the 22nd of November after helping in the liberation of your town, my father, Jimmie Knox, together with his driver Kirby stayed at the farm owned by the Peeters family on the Lange Heide.*
>
> *The following morning the 23rd which was wet and dismal not like today, the fighting continued.   5 Troop left on foot and*

walked across country towards Sevenum a town to be liberated. On the way they met a group of determined Germans and radioed HQ for assistance. With my father in command, 3 Troop responded to the Order to give assistance. All four armoured cars left the farm and with my Father's car in the lead went along Rozendaal towards Sevenum.

They had not gone far when his car ran over a group of mines. My father suffered a cut knee, his gunner was also injured and in the words of my father "Regrettably my driver Kirby did not fare well"

My father hitched a ride on the following armoured car. In less than two kilometres that too ran over some more mines and this time he suffered a serious and nearly fatal head injury. Which he, in his modesty, just called a "dented head".

The rest of the troop then continued and successfully convinced the determined Germans to give up.

On the following Tuesday night of 28th/29th November near Boekend three members of 7 Troop were in the wrong place at the wrong time. Lieutenant Tallack, Sergeant Gatenby and Trooper Gore were all killed when a shell landed on their headquarters.

Of the 150 soldiers of "C" Squadron that had landed in Normandy by the time Holland had been liberated over 100 had been wounded, and of the 35 that had been killed in action, there are 4 who together with Lieutenant Pear and Sergeant Watson now rest here before us under the ground they fought to liberate.

I know that I can speak for my father and I believe that the entire 49th Recce felt the same. They all volunteered to be here, in a foreign land a long way from home, to FIGHT so that you could be FREE to LIVE, LOVE, LAUGH and be HAPPY in a land that you can call your own.

If these Polar Bears could speak to us today they would say how pleased and secretly proud they are that you still look after their graves and remember the sacrifices made by the Polar Bears. For that, we, their children, grandchildren and now their great-grandchildren say a very, very sincere thank you.

A Story Committed to History

Roll of Honour

Name	Rank	Service Number	Date Of Death	Age	Battle	Grave Ref.	Cemetery Name
Chevinsky, Woolf Barnett	Trooper	4617835	08/03/1945	24	De Temple	14. B. 10.	Arnhem Oosterbeek War Cemetery
Brown, Leslie Cyril	Trooper	14317769	21/08/1944	20	La Roque	XII. F. 14.	Banneville-La-Campagne War Cemetery
Neal, Thomas Newbigging	Trooper	3606690	23/08/1944	21	Norolles	XII. F. 15.	Banneville-La-Campagne War Cemetery
Duquemin, Albert Herbert	Private	2736234	02/08/1944	25	Touffreville	Xii. A. 21.	Bayeux War Cemetery
Greenwood, John Walter Reginald	Trooper	7948739	12/08/1944	20	Bellengreville	Xii. A. 2.	Bayeux War Cemetery

Roll of Honour

Appendix I

Name	Rank	Service Number	Date Of Death	Age	Battle	Grave Ref.	Cemetery Name
Pettit, Walter Henry	Sergeant	1080943	02/08/1944	32	Touffreville	Xii. A. 10.	Bayeux War Cemetery
Pickford, Gordon Maitland	Sergeant	2609858	16/08/1944	34	Mezidon	Xii. A. 4.	Bayeux War Cemetery
Wood, George William	Trooper	2658907	10/08/1944	25	Chicheboville	Xii. A. 3.	Bayeux War Cemetery
Collins, John William	Lance Sergeant	6351690	06/10/1944	30	Tilburg	19. A. 1.	Bergen-Op-Zoom War Cemetery
Murrell, Alfred James	Trooper	5836493	28/10/1944	22	Wouw	7. C. 21.	Bergen-Op-Zoom War Cemetery
Wright, Arthur Joseph Jellicoe	Trooper	6349130	28/10/1944	29	Wouw	7. C. 18.	Bergen-Op-Zoom War Cemetery

Roll of Honour

Appendix I

Name	Rank	Service Number	Date Of Death	Age	Battle	Grave Ref.	Cemetery Name
Doran, Alexander Miller	Trooper	14397222	24/08/1944	?	Norolles	2. J. 14.	Hermanville War Cemetery
Briston, Joseph Graham	Trooper	3307685	26/01/1945	37	De Temple	7. G. 7.	Jonkerbos War Cemetery
Thomas, David Ronald	Corporal	3060026	12/03/1945	25	Hien	7. D. 3.	Jonkerbos War Cemetery
Thomas, Eric Kelvyn	Trooper	14401446	26/01/1945	19	De Temple	7. G. 6.	Jonkerbos War Cemetery
Arran, Ralph	Corporal	14404454	16/10/1944	20	Ryckevorsa I	II. C. 6.	Leopoldsburg War Cemetery
Baker, Cyril	Trooper	14201709	06/10/1944	21	Tilburg	III. B. 5.	Leopoldsburg War Cemetery
Martin, Wilfred	Sergeant	2655296	04/10/1944	?	United Kingdom	II. C. 2.	Leopoldsburg War Cemetery

Roll of Honour

Appendix I

Name	Rank	Service Number	Date Of Death	Age	Battle	Grave Ref.	Cemetery Name
Tallack, John Basil	Lieutenant	314967	28/11/1944	20	Blerick	Row 2. Grave 2.	Maasbree RC Cemetery
Gatenby, Frank	Sergeant	2656000	29/11/1944	36	Blerick	Row 2. Grave 3.	Maasbree RC Cemetery
Gore, John James	Trooper	5835887	29/11/1944	22	Blerick	Row 2. Grave 1.	Maasbree RC Cemetery
Kirby, Cecil Ernest	Trooper	2618216	23/11/1944	24	Maasbree	Row 2. Grave 4.	Maasbree RC Cemetery
Hurley, Donald William	Trooper	3777179	17/11/1944	22	Antwerp	I. E. 2.	Schoonselhof Cemetery
Starky James Philip	Trooper	4757978	11/11/1944	22	Antwerp	III. D.18.	Schoonselhof Cemetery

"C" Squadron Cemeteries

Arnhem Oosterbeek War Cemetery

Arnhem is in the eastern Netherlands. Oosterbeek lies 7 Kms west of Arnhem on the road to Wageningen. From the Utrechtseweg, turn on to the Stationsweg heading for Oosterbeek Station. At the railway station, turn right on to Van Limburg Stirumweg. The entrance to the cemetery is a short distance along this road opposite the town cemetery.

Banneville-la-Campagne War Cemetery

Banneville-la-Campagne is a village in Normandy, which is 10 kilometres east of Caen. The cemetery lies 100 metres south of the main road (the N175) between Caen and Pont L'Eveque, about 8 kilometres east of Caen.

Bayeux War Cemetery

The town of Bayeux, in Normandy, is 24 kilometres northwest of Caen. Bayeux War Cemetery is situated in the southwestern outskirts of the town on the by-pass, which is named Rue de Sir Fabian Ware. On the opposite side of the road stands the Bayeux Memorial.

Bergen-op-Zoom War Cemetery

Bergen-op-Zoom is a town in the Dutch province of Noord-Brabant, 40 kilometres northwest of Antwerp (Belgium). Bergen-op-Zoom War Cemetery and Bergen-op-Zoom Canadian War Cemetery are almost next to one another, 3 kilometres east of the town centre, on a road named Ruytershoveweg, which runs parallel with the A58 Bergen-op-Zoom to Roosendaal motorway.

The cemeteries can be reached from the motorway by taking the Bergen-op-Zoom exit, which leads on to Rooseveltlaan. At the first crossroads the cemeteries are signposted to the right. There is a further signposted right turn after 1 kilometre, and the cemeteries are 2 kilometres along this road on the left-hand side.

Druten (Puiflijk) Roman Catholic Churchyard

The hamlet of Puiflijk is 2 kilometres southwest of Druten and about 22 kilometres west of Nijmegen, which is the nearest convenient centre. The churchyard is in the centre of Puiflijk. The war graves are against the western boundary wall near the entrance.

Etreville Churchyard

Etreville is a village and commune about 53 kilometres northwest of Evreux. The cemetery is about 2 kilometres north of the main road from Pont-Audemer to Rouen (N.180). Some 12 yards south-west of the church are the graves of one soldier and two airmen belonging to the forces of the United Kingdom and two airmen of the Royal Canadian Air Force.

Herman War Cemetery

Hermanville-sur-Mer lies 13 kilometres north of Caen on the road to Lion-sur-Mer (the D60). To reach the War Cemetery go northwards right through Hermanville; after leaving the Mairie (Town Hall) on your left, turn right. The gates to the War Cemetery will be found after 300 metres.

Jonkerbos War Cemetery

The town of Nijmegen is located south of Arnhem and Jonkerbos War Cemetery is situated in the south west part of the town. From the A73/E31 motorway turn off at "Knooppunt Lindenholt", the junction with the A326/N326. Follow the N326 in the direction of Nijmegen over two roundabouts to a crossroads and at the crossroads turn right into Weg Door Jonkerbos. Follow this road under the railway and round a right-hand bend. Just after the bend turn left into Burgemeester Daleslaan and the cemetery is a short way along here on the right.

Leopoldsburg War Cemetery

Leopoldsburg (also known as Bourg-Leopold) is located 58 km northeast of Leuven on the N73. Follow the N73 into Leopoldsburg town centre. Follow the one-way system around the town and at the junction of the Koning Albert I Plein the cemetery is signposted. Follow the direction of the signpost to the right into Koning Albert I Plein. At the crossroads turn left into Priester Poppelaan and at the T junction turn right into Koning Leopold III Laan. At the crossroads turn left into Koning Leopold II Laan and the cemetery is sited 200 metres along on the right.

Lieurey Communal Cemetery

The village and commune of Lieurey lie about 15 kilometres south of Pont-Audemer. The cemetery is northwest of the village, 400 yards down a track that runs between the N.810 road from Pont-Audemer and the D.137 road to St. Georges. Adjacent to the north wall, and some 21 yards from the north-western corner of the cemetery, are the graves of four Commonwealth soldiers.

Maasbree Roman Catholic Cemetery

Maasbree is a village of Limburg, 8 kilometres west of Venlo on the road to Helmond. Venlo is the nearest convenient centre. The cemetery is situated on Achter de Hoven some 180 metres north of the parish church, which stands in the centre of the village; the graves are to the east side of a large memorial in the centre of the burial ground.

Schoonselhof Cemetery

Antwerp lies 57 Km north of Brussels on the E19 and 59 km north east of Gent on the E17 motorway. The cemetery itself is located in Wilrijk, a suburb of Antwerp. From the Bistplein in front of the railway station in Wilrijk follow the Kleinsteenweg for 300 M until you arrive at the ring road. Turn right and follow the ring road for 100 M to the first set of traffic lights and turn left. Go under the flyover and continue straight on over the dual carriageway into Jules Moretus Lei. Follow this street for 1 kilometre and the entrance to the Municipal Cemetery is on your left. After entering the cemetery follow the Commission signs to the three Commission plots at the far end of the cemetery. Alternatively ask for their location at the office within the cemetery.

Another Read

Books by the same author

The Abattoir.

The story about a man who thinks that murder is not murder if you can't find the body. Is he proved right?

ISBN   9798603855387

The Only Way is Down

What happens when the rule book doesn't cover what goes wrong at 35,000 feet.

ISBN   9798668122127

A Time in Hell

The second in the Peter Knight adventure series where he becomes involved in a vendetta. He helps to neutralise the situation and seeks to achieve Tara's release from hell.

ISBN   9798545886548

In the Footsteps of a POLAR BEAR

A tribute to Captain J. E. Knox his exploits in life and with the 49th (West Riding) Recce during WW2

ISBN   9798567071908

Printed in Great Britain
by Amazon